Advance praise for *Consider the Butterfly:*

"This delightful book of magical stories will make you laugh, cry, and call your friends to share the blessing. It is a potent reminder of the Divine grace that always operates unseen, and the special moments when it is so clearly revealed. Carol Lynn Pearson has written one of those rare books with the power to remind us of what life is all about. You'll want to buy a carton and give them to all the people who are precious to you."
—**Joan Borysenko, Ph.D.,** author of *Inner Peace for Busy People* and *A Pocketful of Miracles*

"A beautiful collection of heartwarming stories. Highly and enthusiastically recommended."
—**Richard Carlson,** author of the *Don't Sweat the Small Stuff* series

"Consider the Butterfly is a gentle and touching work and gives a large measure of reassurance to anyone who reads it. With a few people of consciousness at this depth, we may survive these difficult days."
—**Robert A. Johnson,** author of *He: Understanding Masculine Psychology, She: Understanding Feminine Psychology,* and *We: Understanding the Psychology of Romantic Love*

"In Consider the Butterfly, *Carol Lynn Pearson reveals how synchronicities—those meaningful coincidences that stop us dead in our tracks—help us contact the magical, spiritual side of life."*
—**Larry Dossey, M.D.,** author of *Healing Beyond the Body, Reinventing Medicine,* and *Healing Words*

"In Consider the Butterfly, *Carol Lynn Pearson serves up delicious morsels of everyday miracles that remind us of the mystery and magic that permeate the universe."*
—**David Simon, M.D.,** co-founder, the Chopra Center for Well Being, author of *Return to Wholeness*

"What a beautiful gift of Divine Love is Carol Lynn Pearson's supremely accessible new book, Consider the Butterfly. *I am caught up in the magic and touched to the core."*
—**Christin Lore Weber,** author of *L.A. Times* Book of the Year, *Altar Music* and *Blessings*

Consider
the Butterfly

TRANSFORMING YOUR LIFE
THROUGH MEANINGFUL COINCIDENCE

Carol Lynn Pearson

WITH PHOTOGRAPHY BY
SANDY WELLS

Gibbs Smith, Publisher
Salt Lake City

First Edition
06 05 04 03   5 4 3 2

Text © 2002 by Carol Lynn Pearson
Photographs © 2002 by Sandy Wells

Published by
Gibbs Smith, Publisher
P.O. Box 667
Layton, Utah 84041

Orders: (1-800) 748-5439
www.gibbs-smith.com

Edited by Suzanne Gibbs Taylor
Designed and produced by Dawn DeVries Sokol
Printed and bound in Hong Kong

Library of Congress Cataloging-in-Publication Data

Pearson, Carol Lynn.
Consider the butterfly : transforming your life through meaningful
coincidence / Carol Lynn Pearson ; photographs by Sandy Wells.—1st ed.
      p. cm.
   ISBN 1-58685-176-4
   1. Coincidence—Religious aspects. 2. Pearson, Carol Lynn. I. Title.
BL625.93 .P43 2002
122—dc21
                                    2002003892

Contents

The Magic Begins

I OFFER THIS BOOK with the excitement of a child who runs in from a morning at the creek, holding something in her hand. She doesn't know exactly what she has found, but she knows it is so unusual, so beautiful, that she has to say, "Look! Look!" She runs to her playmates and shares the discovery in an innocent and awesome show and tell.

I have lived my life by faith, choosing to believe that life *has* to make sense, choosing to believe there is Spirit behind matter, choosing to believe consciousness survives death, choosing to believe there is a God and that God is good.

I remember the day in my twenties when I wrote a simple little verse, sitting on the rocks of the Aegean Sea on the shore of the Greek island of Mykonos—blue water melting into blue sky, pelicans, fishing boats, windmills, tiny whitewashed churches, peace.

I know only as much of God and the world
As a creature with two eyes must.
But what I do understand, I love,
And what I don't understand, I trust.

Trust is how I have lived my life. But always, always, there has been that hunger to *know*, to *see*, to *experience* the unseen world. I have been a mystic with nothing in my poor little cup but trust. How is it that some have held out their cup and received visions, voices, revelations, appearances from deceased loved ones, angelic encounters, and astonishing answers to prayers—big, big things to fill their mystical cup, while trust rattled around in mine?

I had pretty much given up on the idea that I would ever experience the mystical. I was resigned just to sit at the table of my cosmological kitchen, sipping the bit of warmth my little cup offered, still keeping one eye on the front door, just in case it ever opened and my hoped-for vision or voice or angelic encounter burst in.

Now, here's the good part. While I was eyeing the front door, something snuck in very quietly through the back door and tiptoed up to the table, just waiting for me to turn around and notice it. Guest and host at the same time, filling my little cup to overflowing.

This phenomenon has a name, brought into our vocabulary by psychologist Carl Jung: synchronicity, or meaningful coincidence.

I'll let the scientists and the psychologists give a bit of background information.

Dr. Jean Shinoda Bolen in *The Tao of Psychology:*

Synchronicity suggests that the outer world really does
reflect the inner world, not just that it seems to.

Dr. David Peat in *Synchronicity—The Bridge Between Matter
and Mind:*

Synchronicities are the jokers in nature's pack of cards
for they refuse to play by the rules and offer a hint that,
in our quest for certainty about the universe, we have
ignored some vital clues. Synchronicities challenge us
to build a bridge with one foundation driven into the
objectivity of hard science and the other into the
subjectivity of personal values.

Frank Joseph in *Synchronicity and You:*

[Synchronicities] are our own miracles and revelations
that ground us in the Creator, and guide us in
developing a reverence for and comprehension of the creation.
Synchronicity is religion without dogma, wherein all are free
to draw their own conclusions from personal experience.
Each man is his own priest; each woman, her own priestess.

Synchronicity! Ah, that's how I can explain that delicious evening I spent with my college boyfriend when both of our watches stopped. And running into the same man on his honeymoon in New York City *twice*, both of us having come there from thousands of miles away. And my daughter Katy starting her first menstrual period while I was having my very last one (I always accused her of stealing my periods). And that time my computer kept switching into "underline" when I was angrily writing in my diary and practically yelling. And—

What I now bring to the table is my own little mystical cup, a treasure trove overflowing with synchronicities, my personal pieces of cosmic wonder, carefully tracked and studied for meaning. In other books you can read dramatic stories of synchronicity striking like lightning, here, there, this person, that person. My discovery is that one person can harness that lightning and use it consistently, daily, for both light and warmth, and use it for transformation.

I began keeping a diary when I was a senior in high school, fall of 1956. I now have a huge shelf of handwritten books and as of tonight—well, let me peek—4,512 single-spaced typed pages. Forty-six years worth of recording my life and probing it for meaning.

About three years ago I began to write down events through a lens that I called "messages from the Universe." One day I noticed that something happened that looked like a dramatization of the inner script of my psyche. I had for decades tracked my nighttime dreams and tried to tease meaning from them. But now I saw myself tracking what Jean Bolen calls "a dream that happens to you when you are awake." If there were messages coming in, from the Universe, from God, from my higher Self, I didn't want to miss them.

Patterns are everywhere. Chaos theorists demonstrate through the magnification of fractals the part in the whole and the whole in the part, pattern within pattern within pattern into infinity. And my life or your life? Not a series of random events, but patterned, held together by a magnet of meaning, attracting this experience, that person, this thing, this other thing. The parts reflect the whole and are related as incidences in a good novel developing the theme. Looking down at the landscape of my life as I rise higher and higher in my "spiritual helicopter," I see the emergence of order out of chaos, pattern within pattern within pattern. Synchronicity! Little metaphors in my personal story showing up in bold and italics, saying, "Consider this. Pause a moment and consider. . . ."

Every story you will read in the following pages is completely true. I have changed names and some circumstances in a few of them so as to avoid invasion of privacy, but even in those the synchronistic moment is entirely accurate. And these stories are only a few, chosen for this show and tell from the treasured many in my mystical cup.

And so back to trust. Trust is the ultimate "message from the Universe" that is whispered or occasionally shouted in my ear as I open the daily notes that are delivered through synchronicity: nothing frightening, always encouraging, sometimes hilarious, frequently mysterious, and always, always fascinating.

More than ever before, the Universe has my attention.

And my gratitude.

—♆

Working with Synchronicity

LET ME VENTURE, from my own experience and from the suggestions of others who have studied the subject, a few things that seem to be helpful as we keep up our part of this mystical correspondence.

INTEND THAT SYNCHRONICITIES WILL HAPPEN

As part of your prayer or whatever spiritual ritual you have, request that synchronicity be part of the guidance for the day. "Ask and ye shall receive." But do not strain. Synchronicities cannot be consciously created. They take you by surprise. Let your only concern be that you are enthusiastically engaged in a life you love with people you love, doing the best you can to create more love.

LOOK FOR MEANING IN EVERYTHING

Leonardo da Vinci said that much of his creativity came from the fact that he looked for the hidden meaning behind every event in his life. I now look at everything that happens to me and ask myself, if this event were a metaphor in the poem of my life, what might it mean? What are the layers of richness and insight I might discover if I mine this synchronistic symbol? Tragedies, joys, triumphs, failures, frustrations, crises—I assume that behind every development, small and large, is something else, something meaningful, a hidden gift, that if received with grace and used with reverence, invites me a step higher on my journey.

SHARE SYNCHRONICITIES WITH YOUR FRIENDS

Find a few friends or family members who are open to the phenomenon. Talking about it seems to invite it. But keep in mind that you may want to tend some messages privately.

WRITE DOWN YOUR SYNCHRONICITIES

Keep a synchronicity journal. The act of writing them down indicates that you are taking seriously what the Universe is offering, and the number of synchronicities you observe will multiply. It's not just that you will *notice* more. There will *be* more. Another benefit to writing down synchronicities is that the act of writing presents an excellent context for really looking at the event, bringing it into focus, and finding emerging patterns. Make up your own method of recording your synchronicities. I have established a pattern that is useful for me, writing them in the body of my diary in three parts. To easily locate them, I write the headings in caps, just as I do my dreams. It looks like this:

SYNCHRONICITY (4-13-01): "IRON DEFICIENCY/IRONY DEFICIENCY." I then tell the story, this being one of the stories you will read in the book.

MEANING: A statement or two about what meaning this might have for me, or at least how it makes me feel. Spending time with the metaphor is important in developing the literacy that allows us to read the messages.

ACTION: If there is an action that seems to be suggested, I write it down and make a plan to do it.

Take appropriate action

If the synchronicity suggests an opportunity be taken, a conversation be had, an apology be made, a book be read, *do it. Trust it.* Action grounds insight. But a word of caution. A friend of mine who is manic-depressive tells me she cannot "do synchronicity" because it makes her lose her balance and go nutty. Any of us can go nutty, I think, if we look for omens and follow them willy-nilly. I would never *do anything* because of a synchronicity unless the action also passed the test of good judgment and was in harmony with the same Spirit I have listened to all my life.

Dream experts suggest that we honor a meaningful dream by doing something in the waking world—perhaps perform a little ritual around one of the dream symbols—to bring its energy home. The same advice, I think, applies to synchronicities. Recently, after a synchronicity in which I found that an old bird's nest had fallen at my feet on the porch, I burned it in my fireplace, symbolic of the "nest" image no longer being useful in my relationship with an adult son. The image is forever emblazoned on my mind.

MEDITATE

Plan into your day a specific time for meditation and be committed to it. Meditation seems to open the door to the nonphysical world and put us "in synch" with the rhythms of the Universe. Not only do we experience physiological, mental, and spiritual benefits while in the meditation itself, but we come back from our spiritual interval "trailing clouds of glory" that manifest in numerous ways, one of which seems to be living a more synchronous life.

BE LIGHTHEARTED AND TRUSTING

What if God wants to play with us as well as work with us? What if God actually wants us to laugh? I have long known that I *am* that I might have joy. Why is it so hard to live that knowledge? Gratefully, it gets easier as I open the messages whose constant theme is comfort. Deepak Chopra says on his *SynchroDestiny* tapes:

According to Vedanta (Hindu teaching), there are only two symptoms of enlightenment, just two indications that a transformation is taking place within you toward a higher consciousness. The first symptom is that you stop worrying. Things don't bother you anymore. You become light-hearted and full of joy. The second symptom is that you encounter more and more meaningful coincidences in your life, more and more synchronicities. And this accelerates to the point where you actually experience the miraculous.

—∽

Family

GOD PLANTS US EACH *in the right garden, I think, a place that presents just enough sun and rain for us to take root and grow, creating families, bringing together the right people to teach and to learn the right lessons.*

Falling in love, two people at the very same time—and with each other!—what a synchronicity that is. And even if their journey together moves in a direction different from the one they'd planned, it can still be meaningful and fruitful.

What if every network of close relationships—parent, child, sibling, grandparent, cousin, aunt, uncle, friend—is an intelligent, synchronous web that holds us in just the right place, offering meaning upon meaning and growth upon growth, experiences more nourishing than the plates passed around the Thanksgiving table?

Many of my own synchronicities have to do with family. I welcome them as little assurances that our belonging is blessed and use them as little helps in tending this precious garden.

THE PETAL AND THE THORN

"Do you know Jane Olivor?" my dear friend Fred said with awe in his voice. "I just discovered her. How come I never knew about Jane Olivor?"

"Yes, I know her," I replied. "In fact, I inherited several of her albums with all the hundreds in Gerald's collection. He loved her. I've never played them, though."

"Oh, you should. She's amazing."

A few days later I pulled out the four albums. Perhaps I could play them now. I felt my heart was fully healed. The last time I had heard the voice of Jane Olivor was on a tape Gerald had made for me when we ended our marriage. "I want to play this for you, Blossom," he had said earnestly. "These are some of the things I would say to you if I could." It was twenty-one years ago, but I remembered it so clearly.

"*I'm—always—chasing rainbows . . .*" The rich voice was filled with emotion. I think that's when I cried, at the first song. Other songs and tears followed.

"*It's over, goodbye . . . doesn't mean that we didn't try . . .*"

Oh, how we tried! For the last four years of our marriage we lived in anguish, both of us believing there was some way to save it, some way to maintain our family, in spite of the cold knot of knowledge that what we'd so hoped for hadn't happened.

We went into our marriage with so much hope, so much confidence that in spite of Gerald's homosexual orientation, we would be success-ful. We both believed what our church taught—you repent, you do things the right way, God's way, you marry and have children, and you will be blessed. We were married on September 9, 1966. I loved Gerald and his blond, bright enthusiasm with all my heart. He loved me to the absolute best of his ability.

He learned the first year of our marriage that the inner shift he'd hoped for had not occurred. I learned after eight years and four children that there were still not only homosexual feelings, but actions as well. My world collapsed. Nothing existed but pain. Two years of pain in Utah, two years of pain after a move to California, and then the decision. To salvage what we could of the relationship and of our own lives, we had to end the marriage. Divorce had been unthinkable. And it was now the only choice.

". . . doesn't mean that we didn't try . . ."

I sent my chaser of rainbows off to find his dream, so frightened for him. We remained close, he in San Francisco and I in nearby Walnut Creek. The children, confused, trusting, still loved him—Emily, 10, John, 8, Aaron, 7, Katy, 3.

For six years Gerald chased his rainbow. I hurt for him, watched him fall in and out of love. Watched him devote his energy to gay causes. Watched him sing in the San Francisco gay men's chorus. Watched him cut his hair short and wear the gay uniform, the plaid shirt and tight Levi's. Listened to him tell me sincerely, "Oh, Blossom, if I could just find a man like you, I'd be in seventh heaven."

I watched him finally, on July 19, 1984, take his last breath as he died of AIDS on the couch in my living room. I played the guitar for him and sang to him and read him the poems he loved from his Walt Whitman collection.

"*. . . always chasing rainbows—waiting to find the little bluebird in vain.*"

Gerald had asked to have his ashes mixed with wildflowers and strewn on Mt. Tamalpais. Two years later, Random House published the book I wrote about our life together, *Goodbye, I Love You.*

Odd that my friend Fred would mention Jane Olivor now, fifteen years later. As I put on the first album, the notes brought a rush of emotion. Yes, it was Gerald's music, but it was okay. I had lived for a long time now with Gerald's absence, with the bizarre legacy he had left me and our children. I had found a way to forgive the pain and bless the beauty. And now I found myself able to enjoy Jane Olivor because she was, indeed, amazing. Her interpretations were surprisingly poignant, original, her vocal nuances exquisite. I even taped the albums so I could play them in the car.

Some months later I decided to spend a Saturday going through some boxes that had been sitting in the garage. One labeled "Gerald's Dishes, Etc." caught my attention. Maybe there would be some things that the children would enjoy using. I carried the box in and placed it on the kitchen counter. Might as well have something nice to listen to while I work. I walked to the tape deck and turned it on, ready to hear whatever song wanted to join me.

I opened the box and picked up the first item. Well, this can go. A dried rose in a plastic wraparound protector—long stem rooted in a thin little plastic tip that once held water, petals faded a dusty red, leaves brown with a hint of long ago green. Evidently Gerald had treasured it, but its meaning was long lost. Into the trash with it. But something stopped me.

. . . There's the petal and the thorn.
There is beauty and there's sorrow,
And we all must face tomorrow
Like the rose . . .

The voice was Jane Olivor's. The message was Gerald's. Gerald's music on my tape deck. Gerald's rose in my hand. Gerald's music singing about the rose, singing about our life together. The petal, yes, we had the petal. The thorn, oh, yes. If Gerald had been able to speak to me, to remind me, to acknowledge what we had shared, this would be the message. Beauty and sorrow grow on the same stem. And through it all, then and now, we face tomorrow.

Jane's voice and Gerald's message continued.

. . . There's a rhythm to our lives,
There's a rhyme and there's a reason,
And we all will find our season
Like the rose . . .

I have found reason, yes, and rhyme, as I've studied the story of my life with Gerald. It has become clear to me that the themes of his life and the themes of mine intersected in intelligent synchronicity. I have found new seasons, too. I have continued to Blossom.

Like the rose . . .

Months later. I had forgotten. I look now at the cover of the first edition of *Goodbye, I Love You*, a cover designed at Random House fifteen years ago. A yellow background. Two roses, their stems intersecting—one upright and alive, the other broken, lifeless, dry. The beauty and the sorrow.

DEEPAK AND SEASONINGS CELESTIAL

This is the one, I remember, that converted me, the one that turned me from a skeptical but fascinated observer into a baptized believer in the stuff of synchronicity.

I had sent for Deepak Chopra's set of audiotapes called *SynchroDestiny,* and was listening to them while doing my morning toilette. On one particular morning, there came a story that taxed my credulity. One day on his way to the airport to travel to Boston, Deepak made note of a certain set of improbabilities that led him to pay attention to a large sign for the Celestial Seasonings Tea Company. Seated later on the airplane, he began a conversation with his seatmate and, upon inquiring what the man did, was told, "I'm General Sales Manager for the Celestial Seasonings Tea Company."

"Oh," replied Deepak, smiling, "I've been looking for you all morning." They subsequently had a fine conversation about marketing and Deepak learned some things.

All right, that's good.

Deepak then went on to tell how he used that story in a talk he gave in Amsterdam. And then someone in the audience subsequently had a Celestial Seasonings Tea experience of her own that changed the course of her life. Mmmmm. I don't know.

I finished putting on my mascara and reached for the thermos of hot water. Recently acknowledging that I didn't drink enough water, I had started the habit of filling a thermos and adding the hot water to a cup with a few whole cloves or an herbal tea bag or a bit of that hardened Postum, anything to give a little taste to the water.

So, okay, Deepak, I thought, so now everybody is jumping onto your Celestial Seasonings Tea bandwagon. I think that's taking it a little too far—.

Whoa. A thought tripped on its way through my head. What was that little box I had just tossed into the garbage? No!

I clicked Deepak off mid-sentence and ran downstairs. Opening the cabinet door under the sink, I reached into the "recyclable" sack. No way! There in my hand was an empty red and yellow box, "Celestial Seasonings—Caffeine Free–Natural Herb Tea—Cinnamon Apple Spice."

I shrieked, and then I laughed. I was *not* a tea person. I didn't even buy this box. I bet it was given to me a couple of Christmases ago. I was just out to make my water taste better. *And here Deepak had made me climb onto his Celestial Seasonings Tea bandwagon!*

I sat down and read out loud a statement on the box, a message from the Celestial realm.

If I had my child to raise all over again,
I'd finger paint more, and point the finger less.
I'd do less correcting, and more connecting.
I'd take my eyes off my watch, and watch with my eyes.
I would care to know less, and know to care more.
I'd take more hikes and fly more kites.
I'd stop playing serious, and seriously play.
I would run through more fields and gaze at more stars.
I'd do more hugging, and less tugging.
I would be firm less often, and affirm much more.
I'd build self-esteem first, and the house later.
I'd teach less about the love of power,
And more about the power of love.
—Diane Loomans, *Full Esteem Ahead*

A message for me! A synchronistic message from the Celestial realm directly to me!

If I had my child to raise all over again. . . .

My four were out of the house—Emily in Connecticut; John in Los Angeles; Aaron up in the mountains by Yosemite; and Katy, newly married in Santa Rosa. But Aaron's two little girls were in day care right next door at this very minute!

Without even making my bed, I ran next door and walked in.

"Grandma Blossom!" Sydney saw me first and came running, then Sarah. "Grandma's here!" Two very blond, very shining, very smiling little girls, ages three and four, ran to me.

I'd take more hikes and fly more kites. I'd stop playing serious and seriously play. . . .

"Come on," I said. "We're going for a walk in the hills."
"All right! Yay!"
My diary for that day tells me:

It had been raining, and there was mud and wonderful clean air and gorgeous sky and green and sun. We sang and talked and played and made a stage that we danced on and spoke to the creek and to the trees and to the birds and hushed so we could hear them talking back to us.

But what for my own children, the sweet four to whom I had given the best I had over those rich and challenging, sad and confusing, joyful and aching years of being their mother?

. . . I'd do less correcting and more connecting. . . .

I reached for the telephone.

By the time I went to bed, I'd had a conversation with all four of my children. I told them my morning adventure with Deepak, and then I said, "I have a message for you from the celestial realm and from your mother. 'If I had my child to raise over again. . .'"

I read the entire piece to each of my precious children. I told them how much I loved and appreciated them and admired the good things they were doing. I asked their forgiveness for every weakness and limitation I had that had gotten in the way of my mothering. I told them I hoped they would remember whatever I had done that was loving and good.

If it had ended there, it would have been enough. But there was yet another celestial tweak, two actually. As I drifted off to sleep, I thought, darn it, I should have called Terri. She and Aaron were separated, but she and I had often talked about things like this.

Early the next morning the phone rang. Terri needed a phone number.

"Terri! I'm so glad you called. I have a great story to tell you!" And here it came again, the whole funny, fascinating, wonderful story. "Isn't that amazing, Terri? Isn't that interesting?"

"Yeah, Carol Lynn. Yeah, that's interesting. I'm sitting here thinking how interesting that is while I sip my Celestial Seasonings Tea. Every morning, Celestial Seasonings Red Zinger."

The final zinger came that afternoon in my mail. Bills, two orders for my video, Red Cross and Alzheimer's foundation requests for money, and . . .

Oh, no. No, no, no, no, no. I stood holding in my hand something I know I had never before received and have never received since. A very attractive, very festive "Celestial Seasonings Holiday Catalogue."

So that's how I got truly converted to synchronicity. Converted and baptized. Baptized in my very own mystical cup of Celestial Seasonings Tea.

THE WORRIED BROW OF JESUS

Trevor called with an offer I couldn't resist. "I'm just putting the final touches on a life-sized sculpture of Jesus. Could you come over and take a look at it? I like it, but there's something . . . I don't know." I also couldn't resist the clipped and cultured British accent of this sweet man born in Rhodesia.

"Yeah, right, Trevor, suggestions on your sculpture. That'll be the day. But I would love to see it."

Sunday afternoon, I grabbed my friend Mario and we drove up into the Oakland hills where my dear friend Trevor Southey had lived for years. Three decades before, Trevor had illustrated my first book of poetry, *Beginnings*. The beautiful work on the cover, "God in Embryo," had helped the book sell remarkably well and put me on the map locally. Many of his creations are now displayed in my house, including the large portrait of my four children, and an inspiring bronze male and female, *Resurrection*, that my husband had bought for our first anniversary.

Trevor was now a highly sought after artist, flying around the world to do important assignments, his work exhibited in prestigious galleries and collections. The Jesus figure he spoke of had been commissioned by a group of Jesuits in Scranton, Pennsylvania.

We rounded a curve on Leona Lane and I laughed out loud. There they were, Trevor and Jesus, life-sized as promised, standing together in the open carport, surrounded by the ferns and orchids and jasmine of Trevor's garden. The one stood very still, brown clay arms slightly raised, reaching out in compassion. The other stepped here, stepped there, spray bottle in one hand, sculptor's tool in the other, totally absorbed in the divine work of his art. I wondered how many bicyclists had lost their balance coming upon this wonderful scene, or how many cars had braked for Jesus.

"Oh, there you are!" Trevor greeted us with his fine white bristly beard, guileless round face, tender brown eyes, a buttery softness around the middle, and a shiny bald head. Beaming, Trevor put down his tools and came to hug us.

"What do you think?" Trevor went immediately back to his fussing. A spray of water, a press of the tool, a tiny dig. He frowned. "What do you think of the face? Now tell me."

I stood directly in front of the sculpture and looked up into Jesus's face. Beautiful work. Reverently I reached out and touched the wet clay, gleaming in the sunlight.

Trevor fussed some more. "I don't know. There's something . . ."

I studied the face—deep set eyes, no beard, hair short for Jesus, lips slightly open. I wanted to say, "It's perfect!" but instead I said, I'm sure with a touch of disappointment in my voice, "He's very—human."

"Of course he's human."

I sighed and looked again, from this angle, from that angle. "I wish I felt—a little more of the, you know, godly."

"I don't want a beatific Jesus," Trevor said, almost impatiently. "I want us to see his humanity, a bit of vulnerability. And yet, there's *something* . . ."

"He doesn't have to smile," I said, "but those lines, those deep furrows in the forehead. Jesus looks, well—worried. I don't like him to be worried."

Trevor stepped back and cocked his head. "Worried? That's not what I wanted. Worry is not an appropriate expression for Jesus."

"What would happen if . . ." Tentatively I reached up to touch the worried brow of Jesus. "What if these furrows were not so deep?"

Trevor nodded. "Go ahead."

Slightly, slightly, my fingers smoothed the clay.

A spray of water hit my hand, and I watched as Trevor deftly placed the tool, pressing, flicking, pressing. Thirty seconds later he stood back and studied his work. "Ah! Ah, yes!"

"Yes!" I echoed. "That's what I wanted! Oh, that's beautiful. Jesus isn't—*worried* anymore!"

I woke up about three in the morning and couldn't go back to sleep. My mind went over and over the words my son Aaron had spoken that evening. "I can't do it, Mom. This marriage is ending." I had been hoping they could find each other again. I had even used some money to send them on a Caribbean cruise while I kept the two precious girls. After leaving Trevor and Jesus, Mario and I had picked up the returning couple from the airport. "I care deeply about Terri," Aaron had said in our few minutes alone, "but this marriage is over."

Four o'clock. No sleep. Thoughts came like static. They had been too young to marry, of course they had been too young. And now they were too young to divorce. Sarah and Sydney, dear babies. They deserve better than this. I played their marriage over again and again in my head—what if this, what if that, what if they had, what if I had, and what will happen if?

Then as I lay there with my little parade of fears, my thoughts drifted into a different room in my mind. Not the sleep room, but that room where two things come together and create something new. My concern for my son and his wife, for their children, for my own pain, merged with the other experience of the day, that lovely experience with Trevor's Jesus. I began to hear words. The voice was mine, but the speaker was Jesus.

"You know, Carol Lynn," he said. "You were right today that worry is not an appropriate expression for my face. And I need to tell you that worry is also not an appropriate expression for your face. Today you helped smooth the wrinkles in my brow, and if you will let me, I can do the same for you right now."

I let him. I pictured Jesus, not frozen in clay, but alive, extending a warm, warm hand. The hand on my forehead. Smoothing, smoothing. So warm. So powerful. A sweet sculptor in the dark. Bringing peace.

Peace.

HEALING THE HEART

I was reading *Embracing the Beloved* by Stephen and Ondrea Levine, a lovely, poetic book about relationship as a path to awakening, and I had found a splendid passage.

Your heart, like the sun, is always shining. But like the sun,
or the heart, any passing shadow can obscure its warmth.

I marked it, thinking of my daughter Emily. She had told me more
than once about the physical pain that she experienced in her heart.
She had told me, "It's shut down, Mom. All the years of losing people,
the years of being hurt. It's like there's a hole in my chest and it's cold.
It's a very physical thing, and it's there all the time, this hole where my
heart ought to be. I want to trust love, but I can't."

Beautiful, loving Emily. I had watched my child experience the loss
of her father and also the death of Roger, a man she loved dearly and
had hoped to build a life with. I had watched her experience disappointment, depression, and betrayal. I had heard her say, "I don't feel
love anymore, Mom. It's gone. I think I don't care anymore."

An unloving Emily? An oxymoron. I had watched her love grow year
after year. Sometimes, yes, passing shadows obscured its warmth, but those
shadows never fooled me. As a first-grader Emily had instituted the practice of insisting every night that the last word she said to anyone in the
family or that anyone in the family said to her was, "I love you," in case
the house burned down and killed us all, as had happened to a family in
the fire safety film she had seen at school. And only recently, even as she
was experiencing a very hard, cold time, I had watched Emily as she held
the hand of her Grandmother Velma, unresponsive after a stroke. For the
longest time, Emily just sat there and held her hand, smiling at her with
such love, like the sun, no clouds there. How I hoped Emily could shine
like that on me when my time came.

Still, I knew she was in pain, and my heart hurt for her heart. These words I was reading were so inviting, I wanted her to hear them. I dialed and, good, she was there. "Em, listen to this."

The armoring of the heart is a shield against further pain tempered over years of disappointment and unexamined grief, amassed at the "grief point" like a stone rolled into the mouth of the cave against our resurrection.

"Oh, that's beautiful, Mom. Yes, that's what I feel like."

There is an ache at the center of the chest . . . like a compass that directs us toward the path of heart. It is a constant reminder of how painful it is to be closed. And what a wonder openness can be. And how much room for the world there is in the big mind of an open heart.

"Wow. Send that to me, Mom, will you?"

After we hung up, I continued reading and found a meditation intended to help release the pain, pressing with the thumb on a certain spot on the breastbone. I found the spot and pressed as I continued reading. The whole right side of my chest experienced a kind of ache, then tiny stabs of pain. I held my hands over my heart and sent love and healing to the heart of my sweet Emily.

The next day I had a phone visit with my other daughter, Katy, only five months married and wanting to talk about a minor misunderstanding she'd had the day before with her husband Jon and how they cleared it up.

"So this led me to thinking about who do I have in my life that I don't feel really clear with, and there's just two people—Pam and Alex. I kept thinking about them and thinking about them and pretty soon I felt this pain in my heart, a physical pain."

"Katy!" I interrupted. "I've never heard you talk about a pain in your heart. This is so interesting. Just yesterday . . ." And I told her about my conversation with her sister, about what I had been reading, and about the meditation, where I pressed on my sternum.

"That's what *I* did!" she said. "I just listened to what my body wanted me to do, and I pressed on my sternum. In fact, there's a rash there now where I was pressing. Then today I did my yoga class and now I feel something different in my chest. It doesn't hurt anymore. And when I think of Alex or of Pam, there's not the sad feeling that I had."

Within twenty-four hours both my daughters had initiated a conversation about emotional pain that manifested itself as a physical hurt in the heart! My two girls whose hearts I had helped create, cell by cell, whose hearts I blessed every day in my prayers. Our hearts are one. And when a stone is rolled over the mouth of the cave against our resurrection, we will hold each other in prayer and watch for the opening.

"Blow on the Coal of the Heart"

When Rozan called and asked if I'd like to come for dinner on Easter, I accepted, of course. No better friends. No better food. Brad's barbecued chicken was at the top of my list.

"What can I bring?" I asked. "Shall I make my cheesy bread sticks?"

"Tell you what. You bring the Easter thought. You're good at that. Okay?"

Easy. More than once in springtime, just to celebrate resurrection, or maybe in winter—at a time when things inside me were frozen and I could not believe green or life or love would ever flow again—I had pulled from the shelf my well-worn copy of *J. B.* just to read the last scene.

It was a grey Samuel French edition paperback of one of the plays in which I had performed at Brigham Young University, where I got my master's degree in drama. Archibald MacLeish's poetic, modern version of the biblical story of Job. J. B. is blessed with everything—a thriving business, a wife who loves him, children he adores, a fine home, peace of mind, and faith in God. Ah, but would he have faith in God if all his blessings disappear? That is the question posed by Mr. Nickles (Satan) to Mr. Zuss (God), both circus vendors turned divine philosophers.

I played Sarah, J. B.'s wife. After the children have been violated and killed, war is raging, the house has been destroyed, J. B. is covered with boils but clings to some shred of trust, claiming still, "God is just." I as his wife scream, "Curse God and die!" I leave the stage and don't come back until close to the end of the play.

I had gone back home to take my own life, but slowly I walk on, holding a sprig of yellow, and speak to my husband in wonder. "Look, Job. The first few leaves. Not leaves though—petals. I found it in the ashes growing."

I find a stub of candle in my pocket and say, "I have no light to light the candle."

Then J. B. speaks the line that is the line I always open the book for.

"You have our love to light it with! Blow on the coal of the heart, poor Sarah."

"Blow on the coal of the heart?" I ask the question with a glimmer of hope, then add—"The candles in churches are out. The lights have gone out in the sky. Blow on the coal of the heart and we'll see by and by . . . we'll see where we are. We'll know. We'll know."

And then J. B.'s final speech, given "slowly, with difficulty, the hard words said at last."

We can never know. . . . We *are* and that is all our answer. We are and what we are can suffer. But what suffers loves. And love will live its suffering again, risk its own defeat again, endure the loss of everything again and yet again and yet again, in doubt, in dread, in ignorance, unanswered, over and over, with the dark before, the dark behind it . . . and still live . . . still love.

J. B. strikes a match and lights the candle. He touches Sarah's cheek. Lights fade out.

Easter dinner was very well received, as was my Easter thought received.

The following Saturday night, very late, my daughter Emily called, needing to talk about a recent challenge. I found myself repeating the lines that were fresh on my mind. "I have found, Em," I said, "no matter how dark the night ever gets, we can 'blow on the coal of the heart.'"

"That's really beautiful, Mom," she said. "'Blow on the coal of the heart.' I've heard you talk about *J. B.* I want to read it."

I made a mental note to try to find her a copy that she could own. Wouldn't be easy, though—it was a pretty obscure play published in 1956.

The next morning after church, Rozan and I were sitting in her car, catching up. Reaching into a bag, she said, "Hey, talk about synchronicity! I spent yesterday in Truckee with Brad, helping his brother move. They had a big garage sale, and—look what I found. I knew it was for you!" She held up a hardback book. *J. B.—a Play in Verse*—by Archibald MacLeish.

"Wow! Thanks. But this copy really isn't for me. It's for Emily. Last night she said she wanted a copy. And, just like that—here it is! Amazing!"

I mailed the book to Emily with a letter, telling her the book was coming to her by way of synchronicity.

Read the play at some future point in your life when you have reading time. But for the moment, receive as a "message from the Universe" the wonderful encouragement of that last speech. . . . Go forward and blow on the coal of the heart, yours and everyone else's that you meet. And when you still can't see, still don't know . . . still live, still love. I love you a lot, Em. I am very proud of you. Love always, Your Mother.

"Remember Every Good Thing Your Mother Taught You"

Again my son Aaron was about to run out the door.

"'Bye, Mom." He quickly secured his long, full blond hair into a ponytail at the back of his neck and grabbed his keys. Aaron had his father's coloring, *my* father's fullness in his handsome face, and clearly his own obstinate determination to keep his wavy, shoulder-length hair, long after the style had moved on.

Aaron was my countercultural person, pushing the edges. I had let him insulate the carport for a practice room for his rock band. I attended a few of his gigs, shaking my head in bewilderment, but looking with admiration at his skill on the guitar. I did my best to encourage him to stay with the family religion, and knew sadness when I saw that it was not to be. I watched him move into an early marriage and now a divorce.

Hugging him now, I said, "Aaron, remember every good thing your mother ever taught you."

Letting me go, he looked into my eyes. He had my eyes, extraordinarily blue, and his look was guileless. "Well, Mom, do you remember every good thing your mother ever taught *you?*"

How like Aaron, cutting right to the heart of an issue. I stumbled for a moment, then said, "Well, not *everything*. But, yes, I remember a lot of good things my mother taught me."

"Like what?" He sat down on the barstool and waited for a reply.

Grabbing the first thought that came to me, I said, "My mother taught me that when I wash my face I should rub up instead of down. That way the muscles get a little face lift."

"Huh," said Aaron. "I've never heard of that. What else?"

"My mother taught me I should have a lot of friends and not just one. That when someone says, 'How are you?' I should say, 'Very well, thank you, and how are you?' That when bad times come you have to believe that better times are on their way."

"Huh."

"Okay, Aaron, tell me *one* good thing your mother ever taught you. Take your time."

Aaron didn't need to take his time. "My mother taught me that I should leave the world a better place than I found it." He jumped to his feet. The interview was done.

The following morning, as I was getting dressed and putting on my makeup, I listened to an audiotape I had received from an essential-oil company. Suddenly I froze, eyebrow pencil in midair, as I heard, "And of course, anytime you apply anything to the face, you must always use strokes that go up, never down. That way you are working against gravity and helping the skin to stay firm. Always remember—up, never down."

Perhaps fifty years had passed since my mother taught me that little trick, and I didn't remember hearing it again until that moment, less than twenty-four hours after I had described it to my son. I looked at myself in the mirror and laughed. Yes, laughter too is good for the skin.

And the message? Oh, as always, live in trust. I have remembered the good things my mother taught me, and my children will too.

I watch my son Aaron. He still plays music that I don't get. And now and then a word slips out that I taught him not to say. But, I see the big things—his buoyancy, his blessed optimism, his clarity at being in the moment, his ambition, his pride in his work, his tenderness with his two girls. Things like his willingness to stay up most of the night laying tile in his sister Emily's new house, traveling to Los Angeles to help his brother John move, or his concern for his mother.

Yes, live in trust. Aaron will leave the world a better place than he found it.

"Age Is a Work of Art"

Before getting to the story at hand, let me tell you about the overnight cases. Following my surprise birthday party, I drove my sister Marie and my son John to the airport. I was helping them get their luggage out of the car when Marie pointed to a small tan overnight case.

"Remember this?" she asked. "Warren gave us each one for Christmas a long time ago. Yours was blue."

"Oh, yeah," I said. "I remember. Wow, you've still got yours? Mine died decades ago."

Later that night, I began a project I'd been putting off for months. I had previously set a goal to read through all of my diaries before the turn of the millennium, and now it was September and I hadn't even started. I picked up the first volume, small and red, and began reading. Then—.

December 25, 1957. Marie woke me up early this morning to unwrap our presents. There were two overnight cases Warren had sent us. Hers was tan and mine was blue.

Forty-two years and I had not given it a thought. And within hours, I *saw* Marie's tan overnight case and *read* about it. And it means what? That Marie and I are good traveling companions on this short, overnight stay in mortality?

Marie's birthday was the day before Thanksgiving and I was going down to southern California to celebrate both days with her. Birthday card, do I have a birthday card? For several years now I had been trading my books and videotapes for wonderful greeting cards designed by artist Atellier Renee. Ah, this one will be perfect. A flower done in purple, violet, orange, and red, with the statement in calligraphy—"Youth is a gift of nature. Age is a work of art."

"Very nice," Marie said, looking at the card. "'Youth is a gift of nature. Age is a work of art.' Thanks." She propped it up with others on the coffee table.

The day was spent having sisterly fun, doing a little shopping, having lunch, going to a movie, taking a walk, talking, talking, talking, and experiencing at least four synchronicities that made us look at each other and laugh. Evening. Anything interesting on television? A program called *One Hundred Years of Women* looked promising. Seven women over the age of one hundred reflected on their lives over the century. Toward the end of the program, one of the women—tall, slim, humorous, ten decades proudly smiling from her elegant face—said, "Yes, being this old is an accomplishment. I sometimes think I should write a book. I've already got the title." She paused and smiled into the camera. "Youth is a gift of nature. Age is a work of art."

I punched Marie's shoulder just as she hit my knee.

This morning I went to a funeral at the church. Just last Sunday I had given Joan a hug. She was frail from several years of battling cancer, but her blue eyes still sparkled and her smile was radiant. Eighty-one? I was surprised to learn that.

Several people that I hadn't seen for years said to me, "How come you never look older?" "How'd you get stuck in a time warp?" "How come you don't have wrinkles?" When people ask me those questions, I've taken to saying, "I made a bargain with the devil. After I die, he gets my soul, and until then I get no wrinkles. Good, huh?"

But, no. The devil doesn't help you age well. To make aging a work of art, we go the other way, the godly way. So many faces I have seen, full of wrinkles, framed by silver, shining, something divine there. Like the elderly couple behind me a few months ago in the grocery store, especially the husband, whose face seemed etched in joy. I could not take my eyes off the man, and I actually said to his wife, "Where in the world did you get this incredibly beautiful man? I want to find one just like him." They both laughed and the beauty multiplied.

My cousin Helen finally gave me a copy of that great photograph of her mother, my Aunt Mamie, lighted somehow to show hundreds of wrinkles on a face just breaking into a smile, eyes shining like the windows of heaven. I pass it in the hall and pause.

That's the kind of face I want. Sometime. A work of art.

MAMA'S CINNAMON ROLLS

Same sister. Same birthday. I was treating Marie to a movie and she had chosen *Music of the Heart* with Meryl Streep. As she drove, I took out the questions my daughter Emily and I were working on for our book, *Fuzzy Red Bathrobe: Questions from the Heart for Mothers and Daughters*. Marie and I had been going through them and having fun and poignant conversations.

"Okay, Kid," I said, "We left off in the section about food. Tell me, 'What food did my mother prepare that I liked? What food did my mother prepare that I did not like?'"

Marie laughed, "Well, I know what food you hated. The split-pea soup."

"Yes!" I shivered at the thought. "Yuck!" The split-pea soup. Thick. Green. Nothing in it but split peas and water and probably salt and pepper. Maybe some onion, but not so you would notice. Certainly no ham. I had learned that big pieces of ham floating around in split-pea soup could make it delicious. But no ham for us. We ate close to the bone, not high on the hog. I have a clear memory of Mama saying, "Well, if you don't like what we're serving, perhaps you could go over to the neighbors and see what they're having." None of us ever did. Even when what was in front of us was the thick, green split-pea soup.

"So, what food did our mother prepare that I *liked*?" I asked.

"Mmmm. This one's harder. I remember the oatmeal cookies. And when she'd skim the cream off the top of the milk and put it on bread and sprinkle sugar on it. And the cracklings."

I laughed, "Cracklings! Loved them!" That's what we called the little pieces of baked fat that came out of the oven in our little farmhouse kitchen in Gusher, Utah, where we pumped water from a well and heated it up for a weekly bath and lit the four small rooms with kerosene lamps. "But that's not the favorite food memory I have about our mother."

"What, then? I give up."

"The cinnamon rolls."

"Ahhhhhh! The cinnamon rolls."

Even saying the words, I was warmed. Every time my mother made a batch of bread, one loaf would be donated to the making of cinnamon rolls. They were simple and plain, without even icing—just white bread, sugar, raisins, and lots of cinnamon. Ah, nothing like the smell of bread baking with cinnamon. Or dipping the fresh rolls in milk.

Movie starting. Credits. Story begins. Meryl Streep in the kitchen. Close-up of pan coming out of the oven. A pan of—*cinnamon rolls made by her mother!* My elbow hit my sister's elbow as we both poked an exclamation point onto this delicious synchronicity!

And why did Meryl Streep's mother make cinnamon rolls and not split-pea soup? Is the Universe asking me to forget the soup and remember the rolls? Is it asking me—as I asked my children in the Celestial Seasonings Tea story—to forgive my mother her weaknesses and bless all her good stuff? Can I forgive my mother her split-pea soup? Of course. Can I bless her cinnamon rolls? Always.

———

Death and Beyond

A TINY RIP IN THE CURTAIN *that covers mortality, just big enough for a synchronistic message to get through. A large rip in the curtain, big enough for a soul to get through. Death. The huge and final mystery.*

How I have wished I could have a near-death experience without nearly dying. How I have envied those who have had their loved ones appear to them in a vision. How I yearn to believe everything I read from those who visit the other side for a moment and come back with thrilling tales of light and incomparable love.

The curtain is solid as I reach out and finger it, except for tiny rips just big enough for a synchronistic message to get through, sometimes a message about the life that we call death.

KATY'S LEAVING

I write on Katy's birthday, September 7. She would have been twenty-five years old today. Waking up this morning, I knew I could either try to make the day a "regular" day or make it a "Katy" day. I decided to make it a Katy day. I will write about Katy.

I have placed over the back of my chair the blue sweatshirt I gave to Katy and wear sometimes when I want to be close to her. I am playing the CD of swing music she gave me for my birthday a few years ago. I have placed beside my computer a picture of her with her beloved cat Juliet, a picture I see now was taken on the tree I sat on this morning in the hills, invoking her presence for the day. Beside it is the little pincushion encircled by bright spools of thread that she made in Brownies. On it are cutouts in felt—a yellow "I," a red heart, and a blue "U." I have lit a candle. I am wearing the earrings I gave Katy that I had made out of her wisdom teeth, a gift I knew would delight her wicked sense of humor. Yesterday I read in the paper that parents are advised to keep something of their children's DNA in case it is ever needed, a used Band-Aid, a fingernail clipping, a tooth. For a moment I thought, good thing I kept Katy's wisdom teeth.

I experienced a number of synchronicities around Katy's leaving, the first one an odd preparation. I see by my diary that it happened on Wednesday, January 20, 1999. I was in the kitchen preparing breakfast for my two little granddaughters. Gradually I began to notice something strange in the vision of both eyes, a little shimmering arc over to the left. I went into the other room to sit down, closing my eyes. The light became intensely bright, taking geometric shapes, triangles in all the colors of the rainbow, shining brighter than neon. I opened my eyes and closed them. Still there, still brighter than any light I had ever seen.

Suddenly I was afraid. I jumped up, hurried up the stairs, and knocked on the door of the room where my friend Mario was currently a houseguest, glad he was there.

"Mario, I need to tell you what I'm experiencing in case I pass out and you have to call the paramedics. This is either a spiritual experience or a brain tumor." I described to him what I was seeing, then closed my eyes to see if it was still there. Nothing. No trace. "Wow. They're gone. That was so amazing. I swear, either a spiritual experience or a brain tumor. Wow."

Two weeks later my twenty-three-year-old daughter Katy was dead of a brain tumor.

"A spiritual experience or a brain tumor." A dramatic, prophetic message to myself, experienced and spoken so I could not forget it.

Her doctor said it was the last thing he expected, this rapidly growing mass that, with only a little warning, put her in a coma for four days. It was definitely a brain tumor.

And it was definitely a spiritual experience.

Katy had announced early on that she wasn't going to live to be very old. And she never rooted herself very deeply in this mortal world. Her brother John called her a "reluctant earthling." Once when Katy was fifteen, she and I were talking when she suddenly began to cry.

"I was just remembering—how it was not to have a body, not to have hands, not to have hair. I'm up here in the corner of Dad's room like a big eye or something, and he's down on some cushions meditating, and it's the first time I've seen a body, and I think, 'I want to do that.'"

I sat mesmerized for over two hours while my undramatic Katy told me her memories of a time before she was born.

"I'm not afraid to die, Mom." I heard her say this a number of times. "In fact, I'd really rather be over there." Even during the two years when Katy was happily married, she would sometimes alarm her husband Jon by weeping and saying, "I just want to be over there."

On February 4, 1999, she left here to go there. Her two brothers and her sister had driven or flown in and we were all at her bedside in the hospital in Santa Rosa. We sang some of the songs she loved and talked to her, encouraging her to fly if she was ready. Each of the children sang a song by themselves, a song each would later sing at the funeral. Emily sang, "Wind Beneath My Wings." John sang, "God Be With You 'Til We Meet Again." And Aaron sang a song he had written that he later titled "Katy's Song":". . . Up in the sky I see birds fly, they fly so high, right below you. . ."

Katy's final gesture, long after she could not speak or open her eyes, was to laboriously bring my fingers to her lips and kiss them. And now that her difficult breathing had at last stopped, my final gesture was to kiss her long fingers, now turning white, using them to wash my face with my tears. As I did so, I felt a strong bump against my forehead. Katy leaving?

A brain tumor. And a spiritual experience.

There were other synchronicities that surrounded Katy's leaving.

There were her friend Erin's dreams. When I finally located her in New York City, Erin said in tears, "I dreamed about Katy last night and the night before. We were at your house and we were children and you were telling us stories. It was so vivid I wrote Katy a letter."

There was the smiley face. Mario was typing the program for the funeral service on his laptop computer. Suddenly up on the screen flashed a symbol he had never seen before—a little smiley face. I was watching over his shoulder as he gasped, then laughed. "Where did that come from? I've been using this computer for five years and I had no idea there was a smiley face in there somewhere!" Katy often drew smiley faces. In my jewelry box I have her smiley face earrings. Wonderful. A mysterious smiley face right in the middle of Katy's funeral program!

There were the saving thoughts in *A Course in Miracles,* a spiritual text that had joined my scripture study and which brought me great peace. On the evening of my coming home from burying Katy's body in Utah beside my parents, I sat with Emily in my hot tub and sobbed in her arms. The next morning I awoke, saying to myself, I am finally defeated, I am defeated, defeated. I read my morning lesson in the *Course* and was told to trust in the Holy Spirit, for ". . . under his guidance you cannot be defeated." I spent the day repeating like a mantra, "For today, I am not defeated . . , for today, I am not defeated . . ."

There were the rainbows. As I went through my file of Katy's papers to find some things for the service, I pulled out the last thing I had placed there. It was something I had found a few months back, and rather than locate her childhood file, I had placed it here in the current one. It was a picture drawn by a five-year-old on lined paper, an uneven rainbow with a curly-headed woman's face and a red heart above it, and above that, in childish scrawl, "LOVE, Katy."

Rainbows had "Katy" meaning to me. When she was small I had taken her outside to see a beautiful arc in the sky. "Mom," she said in her wise voice, "I know what a rainbow is."

"What is a rainbow, Katy?" I asked.

"I think," she said seriously, "I think—a rainbow is the truth."

A few weeks after Katy left, I saw the Mother of All Rainbows. The night before, I had a lucid dream of Katy. I heard her voice very clearly. In the dream I said to myself, I can't be hearing Katy's voice, she's not here anymore. I turned and there she was. I thought, well, I can't feel her, she's not here anymore. I reached out my hands and grasped her solid arms.

I was telling that dream to my three friends as we were driving down to San Luis Obispo for a reprieve. Susan, Rozan, and Judy had all loved Katy. It had been raining when we left Walnut Creek, and when it cleared, suddenly there was the most spectacular rainbow any of us had ever seen. A double rainbow, utterly clear, luminous, fluorescent. A cosmic event in the sky! Susan, who was driving, could hardly keep the car on the road. "This is Katy's rainbow," she said, "I know it, I know it!"

Maybe that's what Katy was saying to me in the dream. "Watch out tomorrow, Mom, you're really going to see something. And remember, rainbows are the truth."

Last Sunday I went to hear Maya Angelou speak. Three years ago I had taken Katy to a conference in San Francisco and she was the keynote speaker. Katy was thrilled. As I sat down in my seat, I sent out a thought, "Okay, Maya, you have a message from Katy to give me today." Regal as always, Maya Angelou came to the microphone, paused, then belted out in song, "When it looked like the sun wouldn't shine no more, God put a rainbow in the clouds."

It's evening now. I've been writing all day, and Katy's DNA has been swishing against my cheeks. The candle on the desk I turned into an altar with her things has burned low. I don't want to finish this piece.

Even writing about her death has brought her closer to my life.

Katy, Katy, Katy. Of all the available billions, what fine synchronicity brought you into my life twenty-five years ago today? I watch in awe for our next encounter.

"IN LAST YEAR'S NEST THERE ARE NO BIRDS THIS YEAR"

Yesterday I wrote of Katy's leaving. Wondering how I spent that day a year ago, I now open my diary to that page. Ah, yes. I made that one a Katy day as well. And there was a synchronicity that I found delightful.

While getting dressed I played another CD Katy had given me, *Man of La Mancha.* I loved the musical, its sweeping idealism, especially the transformation of the rough and degraded Aldonza into the lady Dulcinea because Don Quixote refused to see anything but her beauty. That image became a permanent part of my spiritual repertoire. I committed to looking at every Aldonza I met and seeing a Dulcinea. Sometimes I succeeded. I would look at the roughest, most difficult people and say to myself, "Look—there's Dulcinea thinking she's Aldonza."

Sometimes, during Katy's teenage years, she was my Aldonza. But we got through the hard times and finally had the clear, sweet relationship I'd longed for. And now on the first birthday after her leaving, the music of the gift she gave was bittersweet. My heart soared and my heart broke.

You looked at me and you called me by another name. . . .
Dulcinea, Dulcinea, won't you please bring back the dream

of Dulcinea? . . . To bear with unbearable sorrow. . . .
To reach the unreachable star. . . .

It was a good day to busy my hands, and I decided to clean out
John's old room, which was to become the computer room. Most of
John's things had been taken with him to college and then moved to
southern California, where he worked as an animator for *The
Simpsons*. Some things were still boxed up in the garage, but a few
were in an antique armoire. Opening the carved oak door, I saw two
large pieces of paper taped to the inside. John's writing. What was it
John wanted to remind himself of years ago as he opened the door to
his armoire and chose what to wear?

Oh, my friend, I have lived for almost 50 years and I have seen
life as it is, pain, misery, hunger, cruelty beyond belief. . . .

The quote was long and it sounded familiar, but I could not place it.

Take a deep breath of life and consider how it should be lived.
Call nothing thine own—except thy soul. Love not what thou art,
but only what thou may become. . . . Look always forward—
in last year's nest there are no birds this year. Be just to all men,
be courteous to all women. Live always in the vision of that one
for whom great deeds are done—She that is called Dulcinea.

Ah. So the lady Dulcinea and Don Quixote, the man of La Mancha, had visited me twice that day. A little hello from Katy, now in heaven? A little hello from John, now in Los Angeles? But certainly somewhere in these words there was a message for now, a bit of encouragement for today. I read it through again, and a sentence stood out as if it had been written in red ink.

Look always forward—in last year's nest there are no birds this year.

I copied the sentence onto four cards, taped one up on my mirror, and sent one to John, one to Emily, and one to Aaron. Katy could read it from the armoire.

KATY'S THREE JUMPS

Sunday. I had arranged with my friend Rozan to use her VCR to make copies of "Katy's Skydive" to give to my other children. The video of this fine event had become a precious possession and had been shown as part of Katy's funeral service a year ago.

For Katy's twentieth birthday, I had given her a gift that made her swoon. A skydive. She had long talked about wanting that high adventure. "Wouldn't that be cool?" she said, with that daring, mischievous look in her blue eyes. "Jumping out of an airplane and just falling!"

"Oh, Katy," I said, shaking my head, "what is so cool about that?"

"Man! The freedom! Just to be free! If only for a few minutes, to be free of all this earth stuff! To fly! Don't you want to fly, Mom?"

"Only in my dreams, Katy."

The week before her birthday, I gave her a note so we could schedule and prepare.

HAPPY BIRTHDAY, KATY
THIS NOTE WILL BE REDEEMED FOR
YOUR VERY OWN
SKYDIVE!

"Oh, wow!" Katy collapsed onto the couch, giggling. "Oh, wow!"

And how she loved it! Friends and family watched as she bravely marched to the little airplane, parachute strapped to her back, waving goodbye. Then the climb to 14,000 feet. The tiny figures falling. The parachutes floating. Which was Katy? Ah, the rainbow parachute.

I paid extra to have them make a video. The cameraman jumped with her, catching it all on film—the momentary terror before it was her turn, the fall into nothingness, the amazed ecstasy of the freefall. And oh, that close-up—a grin as big as the sky, nostrils flared with the rushing air, two thumbs up! Free, free of all this earth stuff!

Three and a half years later Katy was forever free.

And nothing seemed a more fitting way to conclude the funeral service than showing the video. That grin as big as the sky. Thumbs up. Thumbs up. Katy, having the time of her life!

And now, a year later, my project for the day was to finally make copies of the video so John, Aaron, and Emily could each have one. As I walked downstairs to get the precious original, I noticed that a picture had fallen off the wall from the arrangement of twenty or so framed family pictures. My hands were full, so I stepped over it, leaving it there on the carpeted stairway.

Returning moments later with the video in hand, I bent to pick up the fallen picture. It was of Katy, looking about five or six, jumping from a tree branch, holding onto a rope, looking down, delight on her face. I slipped into my "synchronicity space." Three jumps. Three jumps! I held in one hand the videotape of Katy's amazing jump into blue sky, and in the other hand a picture that had somehow jumped off the wall, a picture of little Katy *jumping*! I sank down on the stair, smiling, enjoying the gift.

Yesterday as I was doing my weights and needing distraction, I watched a talk show that had as a guest Char, a psychic medium. "When a picture of someone who is now on the other side falls off the wall, it's them making their presence known," she said, "it's them just saying hello."

Well, hello yourself, Katy. And what? What was that?

"Man! The freedom! Just to be free! It's so great. Don't you want to fly, Mom?"

KATY'S ETERNAL LIFE CYCLE

Not long after Katy's three jumps, I had another "visitation in threes" from her.

It started at the office of my chiropractor. Dr. Carter was a good Catholic man, and often, when we weren't telling jokes, we were discussing religion. On this particular day I was telling him about the novel I was reading, *Altar Music,* by my friend Christin Lore Weber, a former nun.

"There are fewer and fewer nuns these days," Dr. Carter said sadly. "It's too bad."

Remembering something, I said, "You know, when my sweet Katy was just a little girl she said to me one day, 'Mom, are there many nuns left in the world?' 'Why, I think so, Katy,' I said. 'Why do you ask?' 'Well,' she said seriously, 'because there aren't many pandas.'"

Wait, had she said pandas or penguins?

Dr. Carter laughed, then said, "Actually, I've always thought they looked like penguins."

Interesting. He corrected me and I corrected myself at the same time. Penguins.

As I left Dr. Carter's office, I decided to make a quick stop at the thrift store that I sometimes browse through. Right in front was a large bin of stuffed animals. I rummaged around, and my hand came up holding a small penguin with green earmuffs and a checked scarf. Two dollars. "Okay, Katy," I spoke to her as if she were a little girl jumping up and down beside me. "Okay, Katy. We'll get your penguin." I carried it into the store and took out two dollars.

That afternoon I had to make a birthday cake for Aaron's daughter Sarah, now turning six. As I stood in the store aisle holding in my hand the devil's food cake mix and wondering if she might prefer the white, I became aware of the chorus of a song wafting over the store's sound system. "Sail away, sail away, sail away."

My heart froze. I hadn't heard that song for over a year, not since

Katy's funeral. It was "Orinoco Flow," the Enya song I had selected to be background music to the skydive video. Watching the video that first evening, I knew the choice had been a good one. Watching the video at Katy's funeral, I knew the choice had been perfect. A clear voice pulsing to an ethereal rhythm. "Sail away, sail away, sail away." Perfect for that grin as big as the sky.

Standing there now in the cake mix aisle, I didn't move, just held the devil's food mix for three minutes until the song ended, eyes closed, reliving Katy's two flights. "Sail . . . away. . . ."

That evening I hunted through the cabinet where I keep my "holiday stuff," looking for the Happy Birthday sign. What's this sack? Oh, the Easter things. Omigosh, the eggs, those several dozen egg shells we had blown and colored about fifteen years ago on that great and ridiculous year we had kept the Christmas tree alive month after month, changing the decorations from valentines to colored blown eggs fitted over the lights. We joked about having a Fourth of July tree, but threw it out before then. The eternal holiday tree became one of our silly family stories.

But I hadn't told my two granddaughters about it. Easter was next week. Why not haul out the Easter stuff, fill a bowl with the ancient eggshells, and put up those cutout figures the kids had made so long ago? Out they came and up went the figures onto the back of the cupboard facing the family room. A large Easter bunny. Which child had made that? I looked on the back. AARON. And then the big yellow chicken with orange beak and orange feet and an orange eye and a bit of scruffy orange fuzz. Whose was that? Scrawled on the back—KATY. I taped the bunny and the chicken onto the wood of the cabinet and sat down on the couch to admire them.

It had turned into something of a Katy day, hadn't it? Three separate Katy moments, in fact. As I stared at the childish decorations, the three Katy moments came into focus, joined together, and held hands. There they were: a childhood story with the penguin, a death review in "Sail away," and now an Easter moment in Katy's paper cutout. Childhood—death—resurrection. Katy's eternal life cycle.

In a few minutes my friend Mario arrived and I told him the story. As a longtime family friend, he had treasured Katy, stood with us at the moment of her passing, and now shook his head. "That Katy," he said. "She pulled off a good one today. That Katy is one powerful chick!"

It wasn't until I hit his shoulder and pointed at the large yellow cutout chicken that he laughed. I could almost hear Katy giggling too. Powerful? Oh, yeah.

"If Someone Blew, I Would Go Out . . ."

I dim
I dim
I have no doubt
If someone blew
I would go out.

The words of this little verse are poignant ones for me. I had written them for myself over twenty years before when my marriage was in shambles, when I was emotionally exhausted from trying to find a way to keep our family together. Two years later, when I found to my surprise that some life still coursed through my veins, I added a final three lines:

I did not.
I must be brighter
Than I thought.

Useful now, that poem, in another project. I typed it out. Time for lunch. My writing candle was today in a brass bowl on top of my computer, and as I looked up, I saw no flame. Evidently it had burned itself out. I stood up and saw then that the candle, though very low, was still burning. I just could not see it from where I was sitting. Ah, just like in the poem—I thought it went out, but it did not.

That evening my women's group came over for our monthly get-together. For years we six had relished our times together, and tonight Susan was cooking again. I set the table in my dining room and placed a small candle beside each plate. "In honor of the new year," I said, "and because I am the presiding matriarch, I've got a little ritual for us." I took a lighted candle from the centerpiece and lit the little candle beside Susan's plate. "Let's take a moment and think about Susan's light and visualize into her life whatever light she needs for the coming year."

When we had done that, Susan took her candle, lit Rozan's, and we did the same visualization for her. Rozan then took her candle and held it to Christy's. But Christy's did not light. Rozan tried again. Again the candle did not light. Smiling, Christy said quietly, "I dim—I dim—I have no doubt if someone blew, I would go out."

The next time my women came to my house was just over three weeks later. They had spent the day cleaning my house and filling the refrigerator while I was in Santa Rosa at the hospital, telling Katy goodbye, touching her for the last time, sending her on her eternal journey. My baby, who should have lived to hold me while I was leaving, now gone. Oh, surely, if someone blew, I would go out! Arriving home that evening, I was greeted with embraces from my women, my blessed women, bringing full circle to me the light I had passed to them the night we sat around my table.

I did not go out. Again, somehow I did not go out. It's been a year and a half now. I must be brighter than I thought. And Katy? She dimmed, she dimmed. Went out? I cannot see her from where I am sitting. Still burning.

Still Burning

After a matinee movie, Susan and I went to visit her ninety-year-old mother in the retirement home. Blanche was losing interest in life and more and more stayed curled up in her bed, a fragile bump under the floral spread. On the way home Susan said, "Mother can't go anywhere, she won't read, doesn't want to talk. I've been trying to think of something to brighten up the room a little for her."

"How about some aromatherapy?" I asked. "Do you think she would notice?"

"She might. Smells so yucky in there."

"Hey, Susan, listen," I said. "I gave an aromatherapy dispenser to

Katy, and of course I've got it back now. Why don't I loan it to you and you can try it out?"

I unlocked the front door and we stepped into the entryway. "What's that smell?" I said.

"I was going to ask you," said Susan, looking around.

"Something—burning?" I hurried into the kitchen. Nothing unusual there. "No, not burning exactly, that's not what it smells like." I walked into the dining room, opened the door to the office, to the spare bedroom, to the bathroom, and the utility room. Nothing out of the ordinary. "You know what it is, Susan? It's the smell of candle wax."

"Well, I'll be darned," she looked at me, amazed. "That's just what it is. Candle wax."

"It's like a candle has just blown out and what we smell is the fresh, warm wax. It is absolutely the smell of wax." I ran up the stairway, opening the door of every room as I moved down the hall. "No," I said, coming back down to the entryway. "There's nothing up there at all. Here's where the scent is the strongest, right here where we came in."

"It sure is. Huh. What do you make of that?"

"A mystery, Susan. We have a mystery."

Moments later, handing her the aromatherapy unit, I stopped mid-gesture. "Susan, what is this thing I'm holding?"

She looked at me, puzzled. "An aromatherapy device."

"And what have we just been smelling?"

"A strange—aroma."

"Whose aromatherapy device is this?"

Susan's face suddenly melted just a bit, as it does when she is near to tears. "Katy's. Awww, Katy!"

I've read of aromas wafting between worlds. Accounts of visions of the Virgin Mary are replete with the scent of roses. I don't know how else to explain what we experienced. Neither does Susan. The other night we spoke of it again and shook our heads, still no other way to understand it. Just a breath of greeting from my little candle that is somewhere, still burning.

KATY'S "MAPLE LEAF RAG"

I did something unusual in my prayer this particular morning. I said out loud, "Katy, I want you to speak to me. Speak to my ears so I can hear you."

An hour later I opened my e-mail inbox to a Valentine's Day announcement: "Greeting Card from Marie." I clicked on it, and animated hearts began to dance to a piano playing "The Maple Leaf Rag." Tears spilled out around my smile. That was the piece I always asked Katy to play. I admired her Mozart, Tchaikovsky, Chopin, but the one I always requested for dessert was "The Maple Leaf Rag." Only an hour earlier, I had asked her to speak to me, and here was one of my favorite Katy sounds. I played it five times before I moved on to the day's work.

"This greeting card will be available for the next ninety days," said the statement with the card. I played it frequently, and when the ninety days were up and it disappeared, I felt robbed, and considered calling Marie and asking her to send me the same card again.

Just a few days after "Maple Leaf Rag" expired, I was about to copy something onto a tape when I decided to check and make sure I knew what I was recording over. As the tape played, I heard Katy's music, things she had recorded. There was piano, ragtime. "The Maple Leaf Rag."

Ah, Katy, thanks. The magical vibrations go on.

―✧

God, Angels, Heaven, Hell

IF IT IS TRUE, *as in the opinion of novelist Anatole France, that "Chance is the pseudonym God uses when He does not want to sign His name," then all meaningful coincidences speak of God and are even spoken by God. All journeys, I believe, are spiritual journeys, whether we recognize it or not; everything we do is spiritual, because only spirit can do.*

And so to identify some of my stories as about God, angels, heaven, and hell is odd. Still, some are quite obviously in the traditional vein of spiritual quest, each to me a testament that the Divine with which we interact is Love.

ANGEL STORY

I had gone to bed once more in pain because of the pain of a child. Oh, when they were little, it was so easy to make things better—a kiss, a story, a Popsicle, something for an earache. But the pain of grown-up children leaves you holding your heart and staring.

The next morning I found two messages in my e-mail. One from Mollie. Subject line: "An Angel Story." Pretty dramatic.

A young man had just left Bible Study, where his pastor had counseled them to listen to the voice of God and obey it. "Does God speak to me?" he wondered as he drove home. An impulse to stop and get some milk came several times and he decided to do it. An impulse to drive down a certain street and stop at a certain house would not leave him. Feeling foolish, he got out of his car and knocked on the door. The man who answered looked at him strangely. "Here," said the young man, holding out the milk, "I brought this for you."

The man took the milk and rushed down a hallway speaking loudly in Spanish. Then he came back with a woman who was carrying a crying baby. The man, with tears streaming down his face, said, "We were just praying. We had some big bills this month and we ran out of money. We didn't have any milk for our baby." His wife added, "I asked God to send an Angel with some. Are you an Angel?"

Sweet story, I thought, and opened the other e-mail, one from my dear friend Christin. She had just read a new story I had sent her, "The Valentine," which appears later in this book.

Dear Dear Carol Lynn,

Busy with something when this message came, I left the reading of your story until this morning. What a synchronicity that was! For

I had awakened about 2:30 this morning in such a state of fear. Night terrors. I get them from time to time. I finally went to sleep again about 5:30—and woke up to a bright day at 7:30. Well, my coffee is perking so I came in here to read your story, and Blessing of Blessings! It is the answer to all my repeated prayers during the night. How can one forget this truth and forget this over and over, I wonder? Thank you for being an angel to me this morning.

I love you,
Christin

Ah, I thought. Lovely. Two separate messages this morning about people being angels to one another in answer to prayer. Not the heavenly kind of angels, but the earthly kind of angels, the only angels I ever experience. In fact, sometimes I get to *be* an earthly one, just as Christin said I was for her this morning.

It wasn't until that evening, as I wrote the "angel e-mails" synchronicity in my diary that it moved to an awesome new level. My eye rested on a sentence I had written the night before.

Oh, bless my beautiful, sweet, pure child in pain. I command angels to be there.

Angels! Last night I had sent angels to my hurting child, and this morning I had received two messages about angels appearing! Earthly angels! And I was one of them!

JOHN'S GUARDIAN ANCESTORS

I sat at the dining room table with my son John, here for the weekend to celebrate the wedding of some friends. Months before, John had said, "You know what I would like, Mom? I'd like a simple genealogy chart to put up on the wall of my bathroom so while I'm brushing my teeth I could get to know my ancestors." On the Sunday that I devoted myself to hauling out the histories and creating a two-page spread of my side of the family tree, I synchronistically heard playwright August Wilson on *Sixty Minutes* say, "If you don't have a connection to your grandparents, if you don't know where you come from, you're in trouble." I was thrilled to surprise John with his chart and he was thrilled to receive it—that rich family history, every branch going back to those remarkable pioneers who settled the West—George Warren Sirrine, who chopped ice from the sides of the ship *Brooklyn* sailing around Cape Horn and later founded Mesa, Arizona—Thomas Morris, who kept a diary of his infantry march all the way across the continent, telling of boiling and eating his second shirt in order to survive.

"And, look, John, here's my grandmother Sarah." He knew her story well, how she left her dolls in Nottingham and walked across the plains at age eight beside a covered wagon. "Just think," I went on, "the DNA of all of these great people is coursing through your body right now. Their experiences, their memories are encoded somehow in your cells. And I think their spirits, too, are hovering around, and that we can call on them for courage and help with our own lives."

"Mom," John interjected, "do you believe we have guardian angels? Sometimes I do and sometimes I don't."

"Oh, yeah," I said. "I don't know that we have just one, but sure, I believe we have angels to help us all the time."

I was sitting to John's left, and as I spoke I found myself looking over his shoulder, and I saw—a guardian angel! No, not an apparition. "Why, look, John," I said, "here's one now!"

"One what?"

I reached behind him and picked up from a little table the antique postcard I had framed at least fifteen years before so that both front and back could be seen. A beautiful, embossed angel in a long blue and lavender dress, with large, shining golden wings, offering a loaf of bread to a weary traveler sitting on a rock. The caption at the bottom reads, "Give us this day our daily bread."

And then I remembered. "Oh, wow, John, look!" I turned the postcard over. Under the green, one-cent stamp was the barely discernible addressee: "Mrs. Sarah Sirrine, Dingle, Idaho."

I pointed from her name on the card to her name on John's genealogy chart.

Are there guardian angels? Can our ancestors be among them? We had just received a postcard from one of them, with a lovely angel with bright wings, assuring John and me and all of us, I think, that our daily bread will be delivered, and perhaps everything else our souls require.

"FOOTPRINTS"

Browsing through my friend Kenny Kemp's website, I clicked on a page he called "Funny Stuff." Likely I put my hand over my mouth and giggled like a naughty child as I read:

Buttprints in the Sand

One night I had a wondrous dream,
One set of footprints there was seen,
The footprints of my precious Lord,
But mine were not along the shore.

But then some stranger prints appeared,
And I asked the Lord, What have we here?
Those prints are large and round and neat,
But Lord, they are too big for feet.

My child, He said in somber tones,
For miles I carried you along.
I challenged you to walk in faith,
But you refused and made me wait.
You disobeyed, you would not grow,
The walk of faith you would not know.
So I got tired, I got fed up,
And there I dropped you on your butt.

Because in life there comes a time,
When men must fight and men must climb,
When men must rise and men must stand,
Or leave their buttprints in the sand.

Oh, very clever! I was actually sort of glad that someone had targeted this piece. "Footprints" had been marketed to death by anyone who could possibly make a buck off it—in frames, on decorative plates, cards, posters, books, T-shirts, mugs, refrigerator magnets.

And was there any truth in this irreverent takeoff? Well, yeah. We can't always be content to be carried, we have to get up off our butts and *do* something. I printed it out and placed it downstairs with a stack of things to be filed. A couple of weeks later I put "Buttprints in the Sand" in my "humor" file, ready for some time when I might need it.

Let's see. About fifteen minutes before I had to leave. What's a good fifteen-minute project? Okay, do a quick sorting of one of those boxes by the filing cabinet. Throw out this. File that. See if Aaron wants this. Definitely throw out that. And what's this thing? I picked up a thin three-by-five-inch piece of wood. Turned it over. Words.

> *Footprints*
> One night a man had a dream
> He dreamed he was walking along the beach
> With the Lord. . . .

Gently, almost as if I were physically levitating, I felt myself drawn into that strange place, that synchronous space where two things merge and the whole landscape shifts. I had just filed away the "Buttprints" piece, and here I was, not five minutes later, holding in my hand the original "Footprints." If someone had asked me if I had a copy of "Footprints" in the house, I would have said, "I don't think so." And there it was.

I sank into a chair and continued reading.

> Across the sky flashed scenes from his life.
> For each scene, he noticed two sets of footprints in the sand,
> One belonging to him, and the other to the Lord. . . .

A scene from my own life flashed across my sky, the first time I read the "Footprints" piece, years ago. It was a small column in a newspaper or magazine. What a lovely thought! I had been comforted by it, feeling like a warm blanket had been placed over my shoulders. I had torn out the little story and sent it to a friend of mine on assignment in China who was experiencing some personal darkness. A few weeks later he wrote and thanked me, telling me he had used the story in a speech to a large group of people and they were deeply moved.

Yes, "Footprints" has become a cliché and marketed to death. Yes, humor is wonderful and there was some truth in the "Buttprints" satire. But I had been directed back to the original, been asked to revisit those thoughts and see them through purer eyes. I am a doer; I don't even waste fifteen minutes, for heaven's sake. I do not think I will be accused of leaving my buttprints in the sand. And yet there is grace. Beyond my good deeds, my efforts, my checking off lists, there is grace. Grace flows in to cleanse my errors, to heal my misperceptions. Grace places a hand on my forehead in the middle of the night and tells me worry is not an appropriate expression for my face. Grace holds me in strong arms when I have spent all my energy and spent all my faith.

I have been carried. And I am grateful.

Dog Poo and Sacred Waste

I was coming down from my morning walk in the hills, a protected ritual for both body and soul. I knew if I ever joined a gym, I might never see green again. Gnarled oak trees, chipmunks, often cows, once a family of skunks, twice coyotes, once far away—I'm sure of it—a mountain lion, always a few people, often people with dogs.

There was one now, a woman with her dog, me descending, them ascending.

"Good morning!" I always spoke to fellow travelers.

"Hi," she smiled. "Great day."

As we passed, I noticed out of the corner of my eye, her brown dog moving into its pooing position. A thought in my mind moved into its judgment position. I hate it when little piles of dog poo are left on the path. Seconds later, negotiating a fence, I glanced back and saw the woman reach down with a plastic bag, pick up the dog poo, and turn the bag inside out. She looked up to where she was heading, then looked down to where she had just been. I could read her mind. "Hey, why don't you give that to me?" I said. "I'm going down and you're going up."

"No, no." She laughed in embarrassment.

"There's a can right down there. Easy. You don't want to carry that all morning."

"You're sure?" she asked. "Well, thanks."

Walking on down the path, swinging a little plastic bag full of warm dog poo, I began to giggle. So odd. *A brand new experience!* A thought in my mind moved into its predictive position. This is so odd that it's going to be the first part of a synchronicity today. Pay attention.

Arriving at the bottom of the hill, I lifted up the lid on the large garbage can and made my deposit. It seemed to be the first deposit made today and fell with a soft thud to the bottom of the black-plastic-lined can. Suddenly a thought moved into its lightbulb position. Oh, wow! My walking down the path swinging a little plastic bag full of warm dog poo was not the *first* part of a synchronicity. It was the *second* part of a synchronicity. I had already *had* the first part!

Forty minutes earlier or so, as I left the sidewalk by the creek to begin my morning walk, I saw a man coming toward me carrying Santa-like a large black garbage bag. He wore a city uniform and was heading toward a parked city truck. "Good morning," I had said. "So *you're* the guy who clears out the garbage can."

"I'm the guy," he replied, smiling Santa-like.

"Well, thanks for your good work," I added.

Now I was *really* giggling. What was *this* about? Something about, as the bumper sticker says—shit happens. And then—we need to take turns carrying it for each other. I carry it for her. He carries it for me. Another one carries a big bag for a whole lot of us. And we thank each other. We bear each other's shitty burdens and we thank each other.

During lunch, I continued my reading in Gregg Braden's *The Isaiah Effect*.

Living as if the world "out there" were somehow separate from us opens the door to a belief system of judgment and . . . we tend . . . to use words like "toxins" and "waste" to describe the by-products of the very functions that give us life. . . .

The holistic perspective of the Essences, on the other hand, sees all facets of our bodies as elements of one sacred and divine force moving through creation. Each is an expression of God. . . . This view invites us to redefine the tears, perspiration, blood, and products of digestion that we have known as "waste" as sacred elements of the earth that have served us, rather than abhorrent by-products that must be eliminated, discarded, and destroyed.

I closed the book, and a thought in my mind moved into a cosmic position. Sacred. Even waste is sacred. All is part of the divine process. I had carried in that little plastic bag this morning a piece of the divine process.

And what about the "shit of life?" We do carry that for one another. Is it also part of the divine process? Everything in front of us, around us, within us that is pain, disappointment, betrayal, sorrow, frustration—part of the divine process? Sacred elements, no matter how abhorrent?

That thought in my mind moved into wonder. And awe.

The Hindus, the Mormons, and the Divine Mother

Rozan and I had talked about going over to the Hindu ashram in San Ramon to see Mother Ammachi, a holy woman from India revered by millions as a manifestation of the divine feminine. She was there for a week-long celebration with more than seven hundred followers. Needing the schedule, I picked up the phone and called the ashram. A woman's voice said hastily, "There's just been a fire here, a kitchen fire. We're closed down. Call back tomorrow."

As I drifted toward sleep that night, two thoughts came together. Fire. A kitchen fire. And—what was that scene I worked on this morning, in my rewrite of *The Order is Love*, my musical play about the Mormons in early Utah living a communal law as directed by Brigham Young. Six hundred people living, working, eating together until . . . the fire!—that's the scene I rewrote this morning! The stuttering blacksmith, who can only be understood when he sings, runs on, trying to get the words out, then sings in loud, clear tones, "The–dining–hall–is–burning!"

The next morning in my meditation-prayer, I found myself moving deeper and deeper into the synchronicity I had participated in. Two religious communities, over a century apart, the Mormons in Orderville, southern Utah, and the Hindus on an ashram in northern California, each trying to develop a society based on love, each disrupted by a kitchen fire.

And then another level of synchronicity emerged. Ammachi is a Hindu woman revered by millions as a manifestation of the feminine divine. Carol Lynn Pearson is a Mormon woman who has worked all her adult life to bring back the divine feminine.

And the meaning? We are One, all children of God. Mormons and Hindus have the same desire to find God, the same need to develop a loving community, the same susceptibility to the vicissitudes of this mortal world. Like kitchen fires. And—is there something I should do

about it? Mormons, Hindus, Mormons, Hindus . . . well, of course!
The Mormons should help the Hindus!

I jumped from the couch and ran to the telephone. My first call was to
the ashram, where I spoke to Ganganath. No, they were not certain how
they were going to continue; they were calling schools and hotels. The fire
department might allow them to remain on the premises for some of their
programs, but everything was up in the air. Yes, they would be pleased to
have someone call about the availability of a church building.

I got out my handy church directory and started calling.

By nightfall I had received permission to offer them several buildings,
depending on their needs, one of them the huge Oakland Interstake Center.
"We'd love to help," said Ralph Severson, my stake president who was
also in charge of that building.

"I think the best building for them is the Danville Stake Center," said
Larry Wilson, stake president of the area in which San Ramon is situated.
"Twice a year we give it to the Jewish community for their High Holy
days. It houses seven hundred."

"Sure," said my excellent bishop and friend, Craig Stewart, "if they
want to come over to Walnut Creek, we can pull all of the chairs out of
the classrooms. . . ."

As it turned out, the Hindus did not have to use the Mormon buildings, but were allowed to remain on their own premises. "We are so
grateful for what you have done," said Ganganath, as he reported this to
me. "Please come over and let us thank you."

I found the ashram at the end of a dirt road. Indian religious music
came from the large wooden building. Hundreds of shoes outside. I

added mine and found a place on the floor at the back, brass gong directly behind me. Up front, on a platform, were musicians and a large colorful banner with a picture of the Mother. And the Mother herself, robed in white, singing, chanting, frequently throwing her arms toward heaven. The hall vibrated with prayers and singing. And then the Mother's devotees lined up for her blessing as she sat on a carved wooden chair and embraced them as they knelt before her.

Ganganath, a tall, thin, American man with a greying ponytail, greeted me with a hug and said, "Let me bring you to Ammachi." The Mother was just finishing blessing a family, throwing flower petals at the beaming group. As she looked at me and smiled, I could see holiness there, radiance, sweetness, beauty, love. She was a small woman, and had a red jewel in the center of her forehead and a diamond on the left side of her nose. She listened to the translator, extended her hand to me, and I took it. She turned my hand and kissed it. I then kissed hers.

"Mother wishes to thank you for what you have done," said the translator. "She says to tell you that you have shown the highest form of love, love that evidences in service. She asks that you convey her thanks and her blessing to all who have been so generous."

I then took my turn kneeling in front of her. She drew me to her breast, rocking and patting me as a good mother would. She rubbed my back, tapped my head, murmuring, "Ponno mol, Ponno mol, Ponno mol." ("My dearest daughter, my dearest daughter.")

Yes, I thought, this is sweet. I could live here.

I went home and called all the fine priesthood brethren I had spoken to and told them they had just been blessed by the Divine Mother.

Each one received the blessing graciously.

The richness of all this goes deeper and deeper. A major metaphor of my life had been translated into a literal event! For years I had been working to "find a place for the divine feminine," particularly in the Mormon Church. And here I had just spent two full days in actuality working to "find a place for the divine feminine" *in the Mormon Church! And I succeeded!* The Mormons opened the doors of the Church to the Mother. And the Mother blessed the Mormons.

One more little synchronicity capped this wonderful series of events. On that first busy morning when I was calling about the churches, I got a call from Karen in Idaho, the friend who had first told me about the holy woman. "Got something fun to tell you," she said. "On the plane I was reading the book I got about Mother Ammachi. Guess when she was born? September twenty-seventh! On your birthday!"

One with the Mother? Ah, thank you!

—☽—

I'll turn on the news while I do my weights and my stretching exercises.

I clicked on the TV, prepared to see yet again the horrendous images of the rubble that once was the splendid buildings of the Twin Towers, and the heroic effort of the workers in New York City. Channel 4, soap opera. Channel 5, soap opera. Channel 11, kids programming. No CNN. Emily does not have cable.

Well, I thought, turning to the bookcase, I'll put in a video. Ah, *Godspell.* I stuck it in the VCR, remembering well the stage play of this charming, 1970s hippie musical that tells the tragicomic story of Jesus and his little band of followers.

I started with the smaller weights, the ones to work my wrists. I stopped suddenly, letting the weights thud to the floor as I saw the opening image of the play: the fabulous skyline of New York City—featuring the Twin Towers! Moments before, I had turned on the TV expecting to see them in ruins, and here they were in the perfection in which they stood two weeks ago!

Reverently, I watched as a variety of New Yorkers hear an inner call to "Prepare Ye the Way of the Lord," drop what they're doing, and run to a joyous baptism in a fountain in Central Park. Then Jesus, with a Superman "S" on his costume and a red heart painted on his forehead, leads his little band around the city, teaching and performing the parables with them.

Perhaps forty minutes later, weights and stretching done, I told myself that right after this next number I would turn the video off and do something fun with Tara, but I have to see this one, my favorite, "All for the Best." I watched as the little group appeared magically here and there in the city, and hoped for one more good sight of the Towers.

When you feel sad—and under a curse—
Your life is bad—your prospects are worse. . . .
Your wife is crying, sighing,
And your olive tree is dying. . . .
You'd bet that Job has nothing on you.

Such fun. So good to see bright, high energy. Song's finale coming up.

You must never be distressed—
All your wrongs will be redressed—
Yes, it's all for the best!

Jesus and his followers strike a triumphant pose. The camera tips, pulls back. Beneath the players—metalwork I recognize. Back further, panning down, down, down. I stop breathing. *Jesus and his followers are dancing on the roof of one of the Twin Towers! Dancing and singing, "It's All for the Best!"* A tiny bolt of lightning hit my heart, a burst of comfort from this clown-savior with the sweet smile and the red heart painted on his forehead—and the one he represented—and the One who sent *him.*

Quickly I excavated layer upon layer of this remarkable coincidence, looking for treasure, doing my own recovery work. "Godspell" means "gospel," which means "good news." I had turned on the TV, intending to find the "bad news." But unable to find the bad news, I had inadvertently plugged in the "good news"! I saw the Towers not only in their perfection, but *Jesus and his followers dancing on the roof, and singing—of all things—"It's All for the Best!"*

I went through the rest of the day wrapped in a little blanket of grace. When Christian came home from first grade (ah, that's lovely, "Christian" means "follower of Christ"), he and I sat together and watched the end of the video. The Last Supper. Jesus looks at his followers and says, "One of you will betray me." Then sadly he adds, "It must be."

It must be? It's all for the best?

Can we take the story of Jesus as an archetype? Can we superimpose it over the story we are playing out now as a people?

Betrayal? Oh, yes. The traitor entered our house and violated hospitality and trust for thirty pieces of silver, coin to be redeemed by the favor of a perverse God.

Death? They groaned and gave up the spirit one morning, thousands of them, and the wailing of their loved ones was like the wailing of the women at the foot of the cross.

Resurrection? After the darkness, after the tomb, the opening, the light, the triumph? I have seen it. The camera has continued to pull back and back. I have seen hearts open with gifts of tears and money and blood. I have seen heroism, strength, kindness, a determination to rebuild, to do better, to become better. To learn more about ourselves and others. But the camera continues to pull back. There in London, the ancient ritual of the changing of the guard is done to the national anthem of the United States of America. There in Moscow, the Russian president extends a hand of friendship. There in the Middle East, Palestinians hold a candlelight vigil. There, and there, and there, all around the world, borders dissolve and darkness lifts as millions choose to stand in the light of love, to enter the dance on the rooftop, to play their part in resurrection. Such good news.

And if the camera could pull back to the eye of God? Could the borders of even time and space dissolve? Could we then see *all*, and in that seeing know that our present pain is labor pain? Could we recognize creation and call it good?

DISABLING ANTHRAX

I stopped halfway through making my bed and stared at the TV. The CNN reporter had just said, "It appears that simple exposure to sunlight kills the anthrax spores, whereas beneath the ground they can live for decades."

Killed by sunlight? What rich symbolism! With everyone else I had followed the bizarre and frightening appearance of anthrax. Evil, I knew, was lack of love, as darkness is lack of light. Where was that written? There must be a scripture. I went to the computer and sent off a query to my favorite scriptorian, my brother Donald. "Hey, where is the best scripture about light being equated with love?" He e-mailed back a page of scriptures about light.

He that saith he is in the light, and hateth his brother,
is in darkness. . . . He that loveth his brother abideth in the light.
(1 John 2:9-10)

Only a few minutes later, as I was preparing for a presentation on Galveston Island, at the invitation of my new friend Sandy, I was looking for something in the compilation of my own poetry. But the very first thing I saw as I opened the book were the words, "light is love." The final poem, speaking of Jesus:

"Death," he said, "is darkness, is hate."
"And life," he said, "is light, is love."

Of course. That's what all of this comes down to: love, light, and life vs. hate, darkness, and death. How could we take all the hate-laced anthrax that is being sent to harm unsuspecting people and hold it up to the light of the sun, disabling its deadly power? And more importantly, how could we take the hate-laced hearts and minds of those who are sending the anthrax and doing other deeds of terror, lift them out of the dark cave of hate and hold them up to the light, disabling the hate by the power of love?

My writing of that last sentence was interrupted by the telephone. Sandy in Galveston, anxious for me to meet a new friend of hers there. "You will love her. She is so—full of light!"

Sandy interrupted my question with the answer. How do we disable hate? The first step must be to make certain that we ourselves are filled with light. That we abide in the light. That we join in the splendid mission of the sun.

"Us" and "Them"

It was pitch black when the phone rang, just a few weeks after the attack on the East Coast. Had some new terror struck? I stumbled from bed. "Hello?"

"Is this Carol Lynn Pearson, who did the video of *Mother Wove the Morning?*"

My video? There could never be an emergency around my video. "Yes."

"Oh, good. I'm calling from Germany. I'm with the military here, and we're having an event for women, and I was told your video is spectacular and I need to order it."

Pause. "Give me a second to turn on the light. It *is* four-thirty A.M., you know."

"Oh, is it? Oh, I'm sorry. I guess I wasn't thinking. . . ."

Groan. Politely, I took her order and, after an irritated hour, fell back to sleep.

Later in the morning, coming down from my hike in the hills, I saw just below me an attractive blond woman I recognized from having served with her on a school committee.

"Well, there you are!" she beamed. "Haven't seen you for ages. How've you been?"

We chatted, then I said, "What do you think about this world of ours?"

"Oh, it's dreadful, isn't it?" she said. "But I see such good things, such possibilities. It's going to bring the world closer together, you know, erase our boundaries. We're going to become one more than we've ever been, I'm sure of it." I agreed. Then she reached into a plastic bag. "Do you like pomegranates?"

"Actually, I'm not very good with pomegranates," I replied. "I find them so messy."

"Oh, that's easy," she said. "If you get a stain on something, don't put water on it. Put on hydrogen peroxide right away, and *then* wash it. Won't leave a trace."

"Really? I didn't know that. Well, then, sure, I'd love to have a pomegranate."

As she placed the fruit in my hand, I said, "I'm so sorry. I keep forgetting your name."

"Renata," she replied, with a faint touch of an accent.

On a sudden hunch, I asked, "Renata, where were you born?"

"Germany."

I finished the walk home, holding in my hand the little red gift, and smiling. Within hours an American woman in Germany had thoughtlessly annoyed me, and a German woman in America had blessed me! We are in such national trauma from the horrors done to us by the intruders, fearfully looking about and identifying "us" and "them." But suddenly I had a bit of perspective. Americans in other countries can be very thoughtless. And "foreigners" in America can come *bearing gifts*! They can even teach us things we did not know! Can speak confident reassurance that we are all becoming closer, becoming one!

I hold the pomegranate up to my writing candle now and run my fingers over the bumpy red skin. The fruit is full, packed with seeds, hundreds of seeds. Packed with possibility.

ONE WAY TO HEAVEN OR HELL

A beautiful afternoon in San Francisco. My ushering buddies—Susan, Brad, and Mario—and I were on our way to usher at a matinee at the Marine's Memorial Theatre. Enjoying the colorful variety in the hundreds of people with whom we shared the sidewalk—the seated and ragged homeless, the sauntering pierced and tattooed and leathered, the focused briefcase-toters looking neither right nor left—we made our way toward Post and Powell.

As we paused on a corner, waiting for the light, my eye fell on a one-way street sign. It had become dislodged and was positioned so that the arrow pointed down. "Look," I said to my friends, "you know what that sign says? It says, 'Go to hell!'" We laughed and crossed the street.

Minutes later we found ourselves walking through Union Square, passing booths filled with art displays, sculptures, jewelry. A religious group was busily hoisting a large sign across the sidewalk. I looked up to see on the sign an arrow pointing directly to the sky, "One Way" written on the arrow, and to either side of it the words, "TO GOD THROUGH JESUS."

Again we laughed.

Within minutes, two one-way signs had appeared, one to hell, one to heaven. I cannot follow both. Going down—hell, despair, judgment, darkness, and fear. Going up—heaven, hope, forgiveness, light, and love.

Signs of the times. Today the newspaper carried more stories of the devastation and fear and economic loss in the wake of the September 11 attack. And more stories too of heroism, global unity, kindness, and determination. My son Aaron came down the stairs after spending the night and glanced at the headlines. "What do you think, Aaron?" I asked. "Is our world going to make it?"

"Mom!" he said with a big grin. "Of *course* we're going to make it!"

We choose the sign that points up. Numerous times a day I join my prayers with those of millions of others who are creating a new thought-form, a vision of heaven and not of hell.

Today, in addition to the global distress, individual people that I love are in their own pain. As I did my morning prayer-meditation, moving geographically across the country, I encountered—along with the joy—depression, loneliness, cancer, divorce, cynicism, financial distress, injury from accident, disappointment, betrayal given, betrayal received. Hell? Or just a dislodged sign? Each person I blessed this morning is a pilgrim, I think, on a sacred journey. I choose for them, and for me, the sign that points up. And for the human family, for our collective soul, only the markers that move us toward heaven.

Do Not Judge

MY BUSINESS—YOUR BUSINESS—*God's business. Often they seem so stirred together like flour and salt and baking powder that I don't know which is which. Wanting heaven on earth, and believing in doing rather than watching, it is very hard for me to stand back and say, "Never mind, that's not my business."*

The following synchronicities brought messages to me that have been useful in examining "judgment" and deciding what is truly my business. Slowly, slowly, I hope I am coming closer to knowing when to take a stand, lend a hand, speak out, and when simply to watch in awe as everyone around me works out their personal destiny, and as the events of my own life unfold.

MY HOMELESS MAN

I hung up the telephone furious with my friend Neal. He had resigned from a well-paying job in the corporate world because it was not consistent with the spiritual journey he was committed to. But now, Neal was virtually indigent. He had not been able to pay this month's rent on his modest apartment and his car was about to be towed out of his driveway. And so on the telephone, I had said some pretty harsh things. How *dare* he go through every penny, believing that faith and meditation will manifest a superior job? How *dare* he make himself so vulnerable? "I just hope you don't find yourself on the street," I had said. "This is how people find themselves on the street, you know. Homeless and on the street."

That was Sunday. Monday morning I found myself on BART, the train that would take me into San Francisco. I was going to spend the day with Sue, to whom I was a visiting teacher in a church capacity, and who was in the hospital there for tests. But I was not thinking about Sue as I watched the landscape of the East Bay go by outside the train window. I was still thinking about Neal, and still angry. How dare he get this close to the abyss?

Here was Embarcadero, the train station I was told to get out at. I stepped off the train. Now which exit to get to the right bus stop? I looked around for someone to ask. No attendant evident. No one nearby at all, except a ragged, bearded black man sitting on a cardboard mat, a white patch over his right eye and a red plastic cup in his hand. I walked in his direction.

"Hello," he said, smiling.

"Hello." I fished out a dollar bill and put it in his plastic cup. I had a habit of giving a dollar to the first homeless person I met in the city and sending a prayer for the rest.

"Why, thank you."

"Can you tell me which exit to take to get to the North Judah bus?"

"Right over there. But where are you headed?"

"Parnassas Street."

"Oh, you're going to the hospital. The North Judah will drop you two blocks away. I say take the Parnassas Number Six. It'll drop you right in front of the hospital. In fact, I'm going there myself right now. Sometimes I watch TV at the hospital for a bit." He grabbed his cane, folded up his cardboard mat and hid it in a little crevice under the stairs. Before I knew it we had climbed the stairs and were walking together to the bus stop. What in the world was I doing? I was walking with a street person just as if—as if what? As if he was a real human being, as if he was worthy to walk with me, as if he was worthy of doing me a favor. In fact, there he was holding out his hand to me. "I'm Rene," he said.

I shook his hand. "Hi. I'm Carol Lynn. Thanks for your help."

"Glad to."

A neon light began to flash inside my mind. "Wake up! Message from the Universe coming through!"

"How are things going for you, Rene?" I asked.

"Pretty good, pretty good. Lost this eye when I was hit by a truck a year or so ago. Couldn't work. Had to sell my house. One thing led to another and here I am. I was head of a drug rehabilitation program here in the city. Have a master's in clinical psychology from Minnesota. Everybody is just one step away from where I am now, you know. You can lose everything. Nothing belongs to you. It's just things. The Man Upstairs gives you the opportunity to accumulate things, but they're not yours. They come and they go."

My neon light was flashing very brightly. Only yesterday I was yelling at Neal for losing everything, and now . . .

"Yep," Rene continued, "we never know what's going to happen to any of us tomorrow. Now is all we've got. This minute. I just take what comes and I keep a smile on my face."

"Rene, tell me something," I said, as we boarded the bus. "You have nothing, but you're much happier than most of the people I'm seeing here."

"Happy? Oh, yeah, I'm happy! All that's important is what happens in your heart."

Rene was sitting to my left. An Asian woman behind me was trying to communicate something to me. "Two quarters. Can you give me two quarters for the bus?"

"Sure," I said, opening my day planner to the thin pouch where I keep my money.

Instantly Rene dumped into his lap the contents of his red plastic cup, a handful of coins and the one-dollar bill I had given him. "Here, I've got it," he said.

"No, no. Here."

Fishing two quarters from his little cache, he reached across me to give them to the woman. "Please. I do this all the time."

Rene never stopped talking. I kept my day planner open and began taking notes as if I had stumbled onto a privileged interview with the Dalai Lama.

". . . It's like we each have a different thing to do in this world, a different point of view, and nobody can judge nobody. The most beautiful piece in all of scripture is First Corinthians, verse thirteen. 'Though I speak with the tongues of men and angels, and have not charity, I am become as sounding brass, or a tinkling cymbal. . . .'"

I had heard these words dozens of times recited from behind a pulpit, but never as meaningfully as they were recited by my homeless man with shining eyes on the bus that day in San Francisco.

". . . 'And though I bestow all my goods to feed the poor, and though I give my body to be burned, and have not charity, it profiteth me nothing. . . . Charity suffereth long and is kind; charity envieth not; charity vaunteth not itself, is not puffed up. . . . Charity never faileth. . . . And now abideth faith, hope, charity, these three; but the greatest of these is charity.'"

When the bus began to climb the hill, Rene pointed out the window, laughing. "See? I told you we'll know Parnassas when we get there. Like we'll know heaven when we get there. Up! Up! We need to keep looking up. Up is where all good things are!"

At the Parnassas bus stop, Rene and I got off together. As if we were old friends, this ragged, dirty, generous, happy man of the street held out his arms to me, and I embraced him.

"Goodbye, Rene. See you in heaven."

He grinned. "Up, up where all good things are!"

Neal did lose his car and his apartment, and he is slowly reestablishing himself in the material world. His spiritual journey continues with increasing clarity and peace. Mine does too, I believe. And, I hope, with charity.

THOSE ANNOYING NAME TAGS

It is deemed inappropriate to speak of the important things that go on inside a Mormon temple, but I think I can tell about the name tags. And my own foolishness.

When I read in the newsletter of the Unity Center that they needed housing for a dozen Tibetan Buddhist monks that were coming to Walnut Creek to spend a week on their international tour, I hurried to the telephone. And to my delight, I got the last two available monks.

I picked them up in San Ramon, Jample and Auteen, slim, brown, smiling, heads shaved, both in their twenties, wearing their maroon and saffron robes. Auteen spoke virtually no English, but with effort, Jample and I communicated about what they liked to eat, about my request for them to call my children and chant a personal blessing for each, and, on one occasion, about my violence. I had foolishly left an apple pie out on the counter and the next morning the area was crawling with ants. I took a wet towel and was sweeping the little creatures away, when Auteen leapt up from the floor where he had been sitting cross-legged eating his breakfast of eggs and bread and tea. "No, no!" he said intently. "Too much killing!" I stopped the killing. (However, in their off time, my monks liked to watch videos featuring Jackie Chan and Sylvester Stallone. Go figure.)

During the week at the Unity Center they created a stunning sand painting, a mandala. Hour after hour with their pen-like instruments, they placed the colored grains of sand, slowly birthing their spiritual vision of peace, while visitors watched and meditated and prayed. After the painting was completed and dedicated, a final ceremony was to destroy it in one sweeping movement, take the sand to the nearest natural body of water, and release it with a prayer that the sacred grains of sand would bless the world with peace.

We now digress to Saturday morning in the "sealing room" of the Oakland temple, where I attended the marriage ceremony of Alice, the daughter of my brother David and sister-in-law Carol. Mirrors on the wall, reflecting back and back into infinity. Beautiful, velvet-covered altar. Beautiful flowers. Beautiful bride and beaming groom kneeling across from one another to be married "for time and all eternity." And—the name tags.

Those annoying name tags! When I had been married in 1966 in the Salt Lake temple, a blue paper tag was pinned to my wedding gown as I was ushered out of the dressing room. "To Be Married," it said, along with my name and the name of my husband-to-be. At that time I was too much in love and too nervous to care about the piece of paper pinned over my left breast, but since then, every time I had attended a wedding in a Mormon temple, much as I tried not to let it, my eye traveled to those annoying name tags. Tacky. Honestly! Somebody ought to do something about it. I briefly fantasized myself walking over, smiling, and unpinning the name tags. Well, no. Maybe I ought to write a letter.

Cut now to that evening in the largest hall of the Regional Center for the Arts, where a sold-out crowd of eight hundred people watched the Tibetan Buddhist monks perform a full evening of dancing in brilliant costumes, authentic chanting, singing, conveying in narration and in scenes some of the history, the religious rituals and the hopes of the Tibetan people. I had purchased eight tickets on rows A and B and sat with family and friends, thrilled to share this fine event.

A dance featuring an elegant jeweled elephant costume had just finished, and another dance was starting, this one in the monks' own "street wear," their maroon and saffron robes. Suddenly, something caught my eye, a white rectangle on the left breast of one of the monks. *A name tag!* Name tags had been placed on each of the monks that first evening, and evidently one had kept his on all week long *and was now dancing with it plastered to his costume*. And not just any monk. *Auteen! My monk* was dancing in front of eight hundred people with his paper name tag on! Well, I should do something about that. At intermission I should go backstage—

It wasn't until intermission that it hit me. Within hours I had observed two widely disparate religious events, a wedding ceremony of the Mormons and a dance ceremony of the Tibetan Buddhist monks. In each of them, a name tag had drawn my attention, distracting me from the larger spiritual meaning, causing me to make a judgment. WHAT?

Little explosions of insight went off in my head like firecrackers. We are all brothers and sisters—Mormons and Buddhists and Muslims and Jews and Unitarian Universalists—all one under the labels of our religions and our costumes, each doing wonderful work marred by occasional errors. Perhaps our job is to see beneath each other's name tags, not even to *see* the name tags. Perhaps I need to be clear about which issues are really important and which are just irritations that are, after all, none of my business. To know when to stand up and speak out, and when to sit down and shut up. And to just enjoy the show.

Jury Duty

Unenthusiastically, I dialed the number of the courthouse in Martinez to get my assignment. The jury summons had placed me in group seven. Yes, I was glad to fill my responsibility, but no, I was not looking forward to it. Probably three days of waiting around and then being dismissed, as usual. Ah, what could I do with those three days.

The female voice instructed me. ". . . Group two, five and six, report at twelve-thirty. Groups seven, eight and eleven, you will be happy to know that your obligation has been fulfilled. You are released from jury duty."

"Yaaaay!" I burst into applause, then grabbed my day planner and stared at the beautifully blank pages. What a gift! Three whole days, at least!

Later, on a walk to the park, I realized the symbolic value of this gift. I heard myself repeating like a mantra, "You are released from jury duty . . . you are released from jury duty." But I wasn't talking about the courthouse in Martinez. I was remembering two small separate events that happened just before the jury duty phone call.

I had watched part of a Gregg Braden video, *Walking Between the Worlds,* and heard him ask, what if everything that happens has its own validity? What if we don't have to judge, but just observe? Yeah, I thought, that's an easy cop-out, everything is just as it should be. What about Hitler? What about bin Laden and the other terrorists? We've got to judge good and bad.

Minutes later I opened my morning e-mail and found a tidbit from Lane, an excerpt from a home economics textbook of the early sixties about how to treat a husband like a king, called "The Good Wife Guide": offer to take off his shoes when he comes home from work, speak in a low voice, never question his actions or judgment because "he is the master of the house." Lane's introduction to this little piece said, "Do we have the right to say this is wrong just because it doesn't fit in with today's standards? I personally don't think we should judge at all. It wasn't right or wrong, just very humorous and sad compared with today's standards." Oh, right, Lane, I thought as I consigned the message to the delete bin.

Very interesting, I observed, strolling now on the path from park to home. Judgment, judgment, let me think about judgment. Quickly I recalled a recent instance when someone close to me was making a very harsh judgment against someone else close to me. "How dare you make that kind of a judgment!" I said, furious. I woke up the next morning with a scripture going through my head: "Whosoever calls his brother a fool is in danger of the judgment." Suddenly two important thoughts surfaced like warning signs on a highway. What if the person who judges is in danger, not of *God's* judgment, but of the judgment *he himself has made?* Wanting to read the exact wording of the scripture, I opened my Bible. Synchronistically, it fell open to where the bookmark was, Matthew, chapter five, and I instantly saw the words:

But I say unto you that whosoever is angry with his brother . . . shall be in danger of the judgment . . . and whosoever shall say, Thou fool, shall be in danger of hell fire.

What if anger and judgment, not God, are the very things that put you in hell fire?

And the second thought, coming rapidly upon the first: What if judging somebody else's judgment is also inappropriate? My anger about a dear one's judging another dear one had been very, very hot. Hell fire? Is hell living not in love but in fear and judgment?

Okay. I had been guilty of judging others for judging. And this morning, two times within minutes, I had been guilty of judging others for *not* judging!

I am a very busy girl! I show up at the courthouse every morning and slap on my juror's badge, hunker down with my pen and notebook, and study everything carefully because it's up to me to render a verdict. On just about everything!

Another "what if" floated through, this time like a graceful bird moving into blue. What if I could feel every day the same elation I felt this morning on hearing the words that gave me back my days, my life, "You are released from jury duty." Is that what was intended by that other message of long ago: "Hi, this is Jesus. Judge not. You've been released from jury duty."

What if I can be very selective and very responsible about choosing the juries I feel called to serve on? What if I can turn all that energy, that indignation, that concern, that judgment, into peace and clarity and use it to get a life?

Back from my walk, I checked my e-mail. A note from Deepak Chopra's newsletter:

. . . And lastly, to practice non-judgment. Begin each day saying to yourself, "I shall judge nothing that occurs" and throughout the day remind yourself not to judge.

Oh, what if?

IRONY DEFICIENCY

It's hard to judge and to laugh at the same time. Something hugely frustrating that has just happened will take a pratfall as it trips over a synchronicity dressed as a circus clown, and then, unable to keep a straight face, will get up and waltz away with a red bulb on its nose.

I had waited seven weeks for the phone call, anxious to get the response of an important agent to the manuscript for the book you are holding in your hands. Finally I called her. *What? She had never even seen it? She had been waiting for me to send it, as I had been waiting for her to respond? I had paid twenty-eight dollars to get it to her safely, and this precious work was lost somewhere in her office? Groan.*

Two hours later, still groaning, I sat across from a nurse at the Red Cross blood bank. "Thirty-eight on the iron test," she said. "Any lower, we wouldn't have been able to take you."

"Oh," I replied, a bit surprised. "Usually my iron is fine. I think only once have I been turned away because of iron deficiency."

Settled in the chair with the needle in my arm, I took out the book I was reading. *Duck Soup for the Soul*, by Swami Beyondananda, really very funny. Opened where the bookmark was.

Irony Deficiency

Here is something ironic: We live at a time when our diets are richer in irony than ever before in human history, yet millions of us suffer from that silent crippler, irony deficiency. . . . not so much a deficiency in irony itself, but an inability to utilize the abundance of irony all around us.

I stared at the page and laughed out loud. *Irony deficiency!* Okay, okay, I get it. I had barely squeaked through on the *iron.* How was I doing with the *irony?* Had anything ironic happened lately? How about my visualizing the agent falling in love with my manuscript for seven weeks when it was lost somewhere in her office? Yes, this day's diet was rich in irony. Could I process it, or would I suffer from "that silent crippler, irony deficiency"?

I giggled all the way to Valerie's office. Then, lying on her massage table, I heard her say, "But in my daughter's new job she'll have to wear professional dress, and she hates to iron. . . ."

"Oh?" I said with my face in the brown leather, "she has an *ironing deficiency?*"

I will not fall prey to that insidious disease. As suggested by Swami Beyondananda, I will process my irony, release my jestive blockages, and pay attention to my humorrhoids. Knowing that non-judgment day is at hand, I will, while I am meditating on opening my crown chakra, also work on opening my "clown chakra."

That love
is all there is
Is all we know
of love.
EMILY DICKINSON

Giving and Receiving

LITTLE INVITATIONS TO PARTICIPATE *in somebody else's life. That's the message I receive from some of my synchronicities. "You are cordially invited to—" Meaning not to interfere or to judge them wanting, but to say without words, "Here's a small gift. The Universe asked me to give it to you." Or occasionally, "This is what I need. Can you help me?"*

Participate in the flow—things, ideas, occasionally money, words passing between us. Such a gift just to be part of it. You can't do everything and shouldn't try to. But you can and must do something when the Universe invites you.

WALLY'S TIE

Wally and I have a bit of a history. We have been members of the same church congregation for twenty-four years, he as an ultra conservative and I a moderate liberal. While my car bumper sticker out in the church parking lot expresses its opinion that "Feminism is the Radical Notion that Women are People," I can be found inside the chapel expressing equally radical notions. Carefully, for I am a Libra.

But Wally and I developed a rather odd affection for one another. Just as the gospel plan would have it, we created an appreciation that bridged our differences and found that being "Brother Jones" and "Sister Pearson" was kind of a sweet family tie. (Oh, that's cute: I just looked at the title of this piece.)

Wally is a six-foot-five bear of a man, but certified marshmallow within—I mean the sweetness that reduces a man to tears when expressing gratitude for his blessings and his feelings for Christ. I was never surprised to learn of Wally's many kindnesses, and grateful to have received some. Such as the time he took a full day off work to drive my son Aaron to Scout camp the day after Gerald's memorial service. And the time I drove up to church in my aging Plymouth Voyager and Wally said gruffly, "Sister Pearson, I don't write poems, but I've got a good ear for cars. Have the oil checked." He was right.

In the last few years I have enjoyed giving Wally a hug in the foyer, and when he hugs me back, it is as if we are both celebrating the triumph of spirit over ideology.

It was the Sunday before Christmas. Dressing for church, I chose my pretty cranberry red knitted blouse and found some dangling earrings of the same color. As soon as the musical program from the choir was finished, I hurried up to the front of the chapel to ask Carmen if she and her daughter would like to come to my home for supper on Christmas Eve.

"How sweet. Yes, that would be great. Thank you." And then, "Oh! Oh! I *love* those earrings, Carol Lynn! I just *love* those *earrings!*"

With hardly a thought, I reached up and pulled the cranberry red earrings out of my ears and put them in Carmen's palm. "Merry

Christmas," I said.

Minutes later I walked into the foyer, giving and receiving Christmas greetings. There was Wally with his arms outstretched. A good Wally hug. Then, "Sister Pearson! I *love* that blouse you're wearing. If ever you want to get rid of it, I'd *love* to make a *tie* out of that blouse!"

Startled, I laughed. "Wow! This is a synchronicity! A minute ago Carmen told me she loved my earrings, and I gave them to her. *Now you tell me you love my blouse! Watch out!*"

He covered his face and laughed as I made a gesture to take it off.

All the way home, I could not stop giggling. Really! I give Carmen my earrings and then Wally—. Another thought dropped into my mind and began to swing like a sparkling ornament. What if . . . oh, how silly! But what if . . . and for *Wally!* It was just too perfect!

Next day, Monday. Rozan's house. "You're sure?" Rozan held her scissors over the pattern made from a tie of her husband's.

"Yup, I'm sure."

Slash. The cranberry red blouse was sacrificed on the altar of Rozan's kitchen table.

Finally I took my foot off the sewing machine pedal and lovingly ran an invisible stitch up the back of the *very* beautiful cranberry red tie, extra long because my Wally is a *very* tall man.

Giggling, we knocked on the door and Wally answered. "Ah! Visitors! Come in!"

Vicki, his wife, brought out some hot chocolate and we exchanged pleasantries. Then I lifted a white box from my lap. "Something for you, Wally," I said.

Surprised, he took it. Opened it. Observed that it was—a tie. "Well, thanks." Held it up. Then— "No. No! This isn't—! You *didn't*—! Nooooooo!" He leapt to his feet, the beautiful, extra-long cranberry red tie dangling from his hand. Disbelief turned to laughter, turned to little drops that ran down his cheeks. "Your—*blouse!*"

Next week at church I saw Wally showing off his tie. I had signed the back of it. And I told Rozan that when my poems are long forgotten, Wally's great-great-grandchildren will still be telling the story of Sister Pearson's tie. And I predict—for indeed I am a prophetess—that when Wally and I share a hug in the foyer, our family tie will be even stronger. It is a good tie.

DeJeah's Sweater

DeJeah told me I could use her name if I spelled it right. When DeJeah arrived at Anderson House, the home for troubled girls that Rozan and I had been visiting every Monday evening, she had only the clothes on her back. DeJeah was a short girl, fifteen, with an air of "don't mess with me," but with a pretty face and an engaging mind. Rozan took her out to buy underwear and socks, and I took her to my favorite thrift store to load up on casual things.

I went up to Rozan's at four to make Wally's tie, believing we could finish it by five-thirty when we had to leave for Anderson House. But after an hour and a half of cutting and sewing and giggling, we still were not done. Well, we'll go see our girls and then come back and finish.

"Oh, let me give your skirt back," DeJeah said, leading me into her room to pick up the silver skirt with the black butterflies I had loaned her for the dance.

"How are the clothes working out, DeJeah?" I asked as she opened her closet.

"Great. Except for this one." She touched a plaid blouse that used to be red and blue and white and was now red and purple and dark pink. "I washed it with this sweater and it ran."

"Oh, that's pretty," I said, reaching to touch the lovely, long, cranberry red sweater with a V neck and collar and silver buttons down the front. "It's really lovely."

DeJeah smiled at me shyly. "Do you want it? Would you like to have it?"

Flustered, I replied, "Oh, no, DeJeah. Keep it. You need a pretty sweater like that."

Minutes later, in Rozan's car, I woke up. What? DeJeah had just offered me her pretty *cranberry red sweater?* And I had said—*no?* Here I was in the middle—literally in the middle—of having such a good time making Wally's tie, and DeJeah wanted to join the fun, and I had told her to go away?

"Rozan," I said in awe. "Something wonderful just happened! And I did something *terrible!*"

"Cast your bread upon the waters," says Ecclesiastes, "for thou shalt find it after many days." Giving is so powerful, so much fun. Receiving is harder. But if nobody ever *received* Wally's tie, nobody could ever have the fun of making it from the shirt off her back. And if nobody ever *received* the cranberry red sweater out of DeJeah's not very full closet, nobody could ever have the fun of giving it, of feeling abundant, generous, powerful.

The next Monday night after we finished our time with the girls, I sat on the floor with DeJeah and said, "Listen, I have the most interesting story. It's about Wally's tie . . ." She sat in rapt attention, giggled, and when we got to the part about her sweater, she remembered. "Well, DeJeah," I said, "I was wrong to give and not let you do the same. So, if you still feel like giving me that pretty cranberry red sweater, well, I would *love* to have it!"

DeJeah lit up like a little Christmas tree. "Really? Okay!" She bounded to her feet.

I've been wearing the sweater as I have been writing this. I think I will wear it to church on Sunday and tell the story to Wally. He will enjoy it. And I will wear it with jeans on Monday night when Rozan and I go to see our girls. And I predict—for indeed I am a prophetess—that when DeJeah and I share a hug, she will grin and giggle, and *that* family tie will be even stronger too. That magical tie.

A BIT OF SPOTLIGHT AND A ROUND OF APPLAUSE

I found myself inordinately involved in watching *The Music Man* at our Regional Center for the Arts, watching through the lens of the horrendous tragedy that had happened the day before, the school shootings in Littleton, Colorado. I was watching on the stage a simplistic answer to a problem that affects so many young people—being marginalized, unacknowledged, made invisible. There was trouble in River

City, and they solved it by forming a boy's band. There was trouble in Littleton, and—it was not solved. A sad synchronicity.

Needing to add my tiny bit to the national dialogue, I wrote a letter to the editor of our local paper, expressing my gratitude for what our theater offers to young people.

> Everyone needs his or her place in the band. Everyone needs to be applauded. Psychologists tell us that to be ignored is worse than to be beaten. People *will* make their mark. One way or another they will demand to be noticed.

> With such pleasure I watched the beautiful young people singing and dancing on the stage of our great facility, dedicated as a sacred space to the arts. I look at the names on the program now, names I believe will never appear in the newspaper for destructive acts. These young people have felt the warmth of the spotlight, have relished the joyful applause of an audience. They have been visible.

> My prayer for every child in our country is that she or he might know the same happy recognition, in a band, on the stage, or in the myriad of other ways in which spotlight and applause can come.

I should know that when you pray for something, the Universe is quick to offer an opportunity to help answer that prayer. The day after I wrote that, such an opportunity came. I was walking down the hill from my morning hike. Suddenly, I saw that the last part of the path was covered with workers, at least twenty-five of them, young people in bright orange vests, clipping weeds. There was their van on the road, marked "Juvenile Detention Facility."

I was approaching the place where the path split. I could take the broad, gravelly path or the more narrow asphalt path that the kids were working on. Better to avoid them. But then—

Everyone needs his or her place in the band. Everyone needs to be noticed. Everyone needs to be applauded. Psychologists tell us that to be ignored is worse than to be beaten.

Okay. Okay. This may be pretty strange, but here goes. I headed down the path where the kids were trimming weeds, walking in the fairly small space right through the middle of the orange-vested young people, deliberately looking each one directly in the eye. "Hi. Good work. Thanks for your help. Good morning. Hi. Looking good."

Some of them smiled back. Some replied. Some grunted. One grinned and said, "At least we're not holding up a convenience store." The others laughed.

"And especially thanks for *that!*" I said. They laughed again. I continued my walk. "Good luck. Hi. Good morning. Thanks for cleaning up the joint. Hi. Good luck to you."

A tiny spotlight. A tiny round of applause.

When I first heard about the Columbine High School tragedy, I thought, Littleton, Littleton, where have I heard the name Littleton? And then I remembered. Only days before the shootings, I had received a card from Littleton, Colorado, sent by a man I had never met but who had been moved by my work. He had learned of my daughter's death and sent a very nice sympathy card. A card from Littleton sent in sympathy for the loss of my child—days before the whole nation sent sympathy to Littleton on the loss of their children.

We give and we receive—performing, rehabilitating, applauding, encouraging, sympathizing. We give and we receive, and as we do, we receive the greatest gift: the knowledge that we are One.

A Friend on
the Other Side

ANGELS, OF COURSE. *And perhaps, guides, teachers, mentors, helpers, inspirers. What if we each have an entourage of beings on the other side that are assigned to help us? Or what if we can invite someone, and that person, as a spirit, can be brought into our energy field? I have a mystery on my hands, and I don't know how to present it here, except just to tell the stories. I have a friend on the other side, a friend from the past.*

EMILY DICKINSON

In terms of writing gifts, Emily Dickinson and I are not even in the same universe. Nevertheless, she and I have a connection. I have always loved her poems, memorized them, read them to my unborn first child, whom I named after her.

When I first met Karen, I was fascinated. After a near-death experience, she found herself to be an open door between this world and the other. Karen was remarkably unsophisticated, never having finished seventh grade. She knew nothing about me when we first met, but said, as I opened my day planner to take some notes, "Oh, I see you do that a lot, don't you? Oh, I see books and paperback volumes around you. Oh, you're some kind of an author, aren't you?"

On one particular visit, Karen surprised me by telling me I had "teachers from the past" around me. "They bring words to you, words that roll off your tongue like water out of a cup." Water out of a cup? That was a little poetic for Karen.

I am transcribing the tape that was made that day, and these are her precise words.

"These are such as yourself, authors . . . A young woman, very genteel, an awful lot of clothing around this lady. Gentle, soft-spoken." Karen described me sitting at a desk, trying to write my grief, and the young woman helping me, acquainted too with lost love. "Strong individual. Genteel, small, fragile body. Brown hair. Victorian. Captivated, covered, held into an area that she wasn't able to release herself. Bondage, but not the physical kind, emotional."

"Was she a poet?" I asked.

"Yes, I sense a lot of rhyming. Yes, she says, you know what we're talking about. The garden. She's mentioning the garden and strolling through the garden."

Garden? Years ago I had walked in Emily Dickinson's garden, and in her bedroom I had somehow persuaded the tour guide to let me have a picture taken of me wearing Emily's shawl.

"She's telling me you know her."

"Karen," I ventured softly, "you're not talking about—Emily Dickinson?"

Karen was silent a moment, then said, "She says her close friends call her Emma. . . . She says, 'The words would come to me ever so gently. As I wrote them down I would think to myself, no one shall see these words. . . . ever so gently the words would fall as water falls from the cup.' She says many of her short script, is what she's saying, now is for all to see, and she never thought that they'd tarry much past her drawer. Does that make sense to you?"

"Karen! Of course! Hundreds of her poems were found in a drawer after she died. Don't you know who you're talking about?"

"No, honey, I don't. But she says you do."

"You've never heard of Emily Dickinson?"

"I know Dickinson's fairy tales, I think. Is that it?"

Toward the end of the "visit," I asked if Emma would be there for me in the future. The reply certainly isn't the best of Emily Dickinson, but it is way beyond my friend Karen:

I will simply impress to your mind
And your heart will take care
And use the stride.
Ever so gently will you glide
Across the page
And make every reverent detail.

Two weeks later, I bought a book of Emily Dickinson poems for each of my children, and began reading her collected works. Immediately, Emily and I began to intersect in small but surprising ways. Here is a brief summary of some of them.

Within hours of reading into a tape recorder one of my love poems "... Has anyone ever died of delight, or do I get to be the first?" I opened Emily's poems and read, "... Than gain my blue peninsula to perish of delight."

After being interrupted in my reading of the poems by a phone call that had to do with an apology and by someone coming by who spoke of having to apologize to a friend, I went back to the book and immediately read, "I felt apology were due to an insulted sky."

Preparing a talk for the Daughters of the Utah Pioneers, I read of my going to my mother's birthplace, Dingle Dell, Idaho, and instantly recalled that the day before I had read in the poems, "For whom I robbed the dingle, for whom betrayed the dell."

Reading in the poems, I recalled a question I had asked of "Emily" in my visit with Karen, and Karen saying, "She is folding her arms and smiling and shaking her head." I turned the page and read, "Gesture, coquette, and shake your head."

Playing for my sister Marie the tape of Karen receiving "Emily," we paused to watch *60 Minutes* and heard U.S. poet laureate Robert Pinsky say of slam poetry, "Well, it isn't Emily Dickinson, but ..."

I dreamed about the Fourth of July, and later in the day heard "Emily" say twice on my album of Julie Harris doing "The Belle of Amherst," "... It is the Fourth of July!"

I gave myself over to thinking about Katy, noting that she had been gone now nearly a year. Picking up the poems, I read, "From us she wandered now a year..."

I e-mailed my sister to thank her for the Emily Dickinson stamp she had framed for me, then immediately went to a church website a friend had suggested and instantly saw the words, "Emily Dickinson Poem Shown to be Forgery."

Finding an internet site called "American Poets," I clicked on "Sylvia Plath." Immediately my connection broke and when I got it back, I found a new face in front of me: Emily Dickinson.

Immediately after writing the word "apparition" in terms of the angel with big golden wings on the family postcard in the story of "John's Guardian Ancestors," I took a lunch break and opened "The Emily Dickinson Journal." The first article quoted a poem that spoke of deceased family leaving behind "Bright Knots of Apparitions" that "Salute us, with their wings."

My friend Fred told me of a synchronicity he had while reading the first draft of this Emily Dickinson section. In the background was "Who Wants to be a Millionaire?" and he heard the question, "What famous American poet wrote the words, 'I'm nobody—who are you?'" Within hours of his telling me this story, I found myself reading in a letter I had sent to an agent, "As far as most people are concerned, I am a nobody, and that's just fine."

After finishing this section, which began with the acknowledgement that in terms of writing gifts, Emily Dickinson and I are not even in the same universe, I received an e-mail from my friend Kenny Kemp, with whom I had never discussed Emily Dickinson. ". . . I marvel at your gifts, at the way you say such complex things with such simplicity. You may, like me, wonder if you really are a good writer in the sense of an

Emily Dickinson. . . . I am so very thankful for you as a writer and you as a friend. . . ." I was reminded that there is a space of sweet intent. Emily Dickinson and I do share that uni-verse. That one verse.

Whatever the nature of my connection to Emily Dickinson, I am grateful for it. And I thank her for having been and for being—an inspiration, a friend and a giver of sweet visions:

That Love is all there is,
Is all we know of Love;
It is enough, the freight should be
Proportioned to the groove.

THE VALENTINE

I can't believe it took me until March 7 to recognize the superb synchronicity that happened the month before. Part of it I recognized. My son John was staying with me during the annual hiatus of the animation industry. I had instituted a "spiritual thought" moment, and that morning I was searching through my *Course in Miracles* to find the place that supports its outrageous and splendid claim that "only love is real." Everything else is sort of like target practice that misses the mark. Here it was:

Perfect love casts out fear.
If fear exists,
Then there is not perfect love.

But
Only perfect love exists.
If there is fear,
It produces a state that does not exist.

Wait. "Only perfect love exists. . . ." That's almost—that's the very thought on—

I picked up the valentine from my desk. It had come today on the fifteenth of February, from Rod, a gay Mormon man who had been diagnosed with schizophrenia and also disowned by his family. He had first called me about three years before, asking me sincerely why he should not commit suicide, something he had attempted before. He had read the book I had written about my life with my husband and felt he should reach out to me. We had had many conversations since then, and once when he couldn't sleep I sang him "Angel Lullaby," a song I wrote while pregnant with my first child. In amazement he asked, "Do I have angels? Does a person like me have angels?" Sweet man. Sweet, sad man.

The valentine was beautiful—cream-colored paper lace in the shape of a heart, with a small pink bow over the center in which were written the words:

That love is all there is
Is all we know of love.
—Emily Dickinson

And now, holding the valentine in one hand and *A Course in*

Miracles in the other, I was deeply moved. Emily's words were a perfect echo of the thought I had chosen to read to my son.

That is the first part of the story. I kept the valentine on my desk, letting it warm me like the February sun making its way through the blossoms of the magnolia tree outside the second-story window where I work. Truly, that love is all there is, is all we know of love.

Three weeks later came the second part of the story. I was preparing a copy of the manuscript of this book to send to Margy in Albuquerque, a dear friend since college days. Aligning the pages, a little pile at a time, I found myself catching a phrase here and a phrase there. And then—.

. . . That Love is all there is,
Is all we know of Love. . . .

That night I wrote in my diary:

An electric shock ran through me! I did not remember, at the time I received Rod's valentine with those words on it, that I HAD WRITTEN THOSE VERY WORDS IN MY EMILY DICKINSON SECTION! *Of all the available thousands of Emily Dickinson words, I chose those to thank her. And those were the very words a few months later she sent back to me in the valentine!*

When I last spoke with Rod, a few weeks ago, I told him he is not to listen to the voices outside that tell him he is worthless, a failure. He is to become acquainted with the voice inside.

"But Sister Pearson," he said softly, "I'm a schizophrenic. There are voices inside me that tell me I'm no good, that tell me to hurt myself."

I had forgotten. "Well, Rod, the voice of truth will speak only encouragement, only love."

Schizophrenia. Rod has it medically. Do I have it in other ways? Does humanity have it in a big way? We are split, I know, ego and Spirit. The fallen or separated self and the Divine Self. The voice that speaks fear and the Voice that speaks Love. The schizophrenia of mortality.

I wasn't going to write today. I was veering out of Spirit and into ego, and I like to write from my higher Self and not from my fearful self. I awoke at two-thirty last night and spent hours drifting in confusion, judgment, disappointment, and a little anger. Drifting out of love into fear. But I decided to write anyway. The bright message of the valentine that came from God, through Emily Dickinson, via my sweet friend Rod, was for the dark times as well as the light.

The thing is, I believe it. I believe Jesus' word that love is the first and greatest commandment, that "God hath not given us the spirit of fear . . . but of love." I believe the *Course's* insistence that fear is part of the illusion. There is nowhere to go but to the safe place, the place of reality, the place of Love. And I am grateful that synchronicities are delivered like sweet valentines to help me along the way.

CONSIDER THE BUTTERFLY

Sarah jumped up on the couch with a book for storytime. "Mine first! Mine first!"

"Mine next!" Sydney hoisted herself up on the other side of me.

"Okay," I said, "What have we here? *Flap Your Wings*. Oh, I like that one."

. . . Day after day, they brought food for Junior. Mrs. Bird got berries and cherries. She got butterflies and caterpillars. . . .

As I turned the page, Sydney said, "Grandma, did you say *butterflies?*"

"Yep. Butterflies." And I continued reading. The alligator finally hatched from the mistaken egg, realized who he was, and went on to live a good alligator life.

"Okay, Sydney, let's see your book. Ah. *Four Puppies*. Love this one. I read it to your daddy when he was little. See? It's been read so much the cover's gone."

Every day the four puppies went out to play. They pounced at caterpillars. They chased butterflies. . . .

Aha! Butterflies in both books, with Sydney underlining the word with a question.

Minutes later, the girls snuggled down on the trundle bed under two matching white down comforters that made them look like angels tucked in clouds. I started to sing my "Angel Lullaby," but Sarah interrupted. "I want the song about the secret garden, Grandma."

I started over, this time with a favorite song I'd learned in church as a girl about their age.

I have a garden, a lovely garden,
With flowers blossoming everywhere.
Where sun shines brightly and rain falls lightly
And breezes scatter sweet fragrance there.

Songbirds come singing out of the sky,
Butterflies winging, hovering by. . . .

I began to giggle. Butterflies *again!* Tonight as I drift off, I will consider the butterfly.

The girls were asleep now, and it was my own face I was washing.
Butterflies, I thought. What fun! And then another thought fluttered by.
What if—no, it would be too weird. But what if—what if Emily
Dickinson mentions butterflies tonight? For weeks now I had been
reading a few pages of the poems every night. No. Don't be *greedy.*
You've already had *three* butterflies. I sat down in my rose-colored
leather chair and opened the book to where the bookmark was.

In the name of the bee
And of the butterfly
And of the breeze, amen!

Oh, amen, amen! When I continued reading, I could not stop.
Between pages 105 and 117, I found *five more butterflies!*

The bee is not afraid of me,

I know the butterfly. . . .

* * * *

The dreamy butterflies bestir,
Lethargic pools resume the whir
Of last year's sundered tune.

* * * *

With only butterflies to brood,
And bees to entertain. . . .

* * * *

Accessible to thill of bee,
Or cart of butterfly.

* * * *

There is a flower that bees prefer,
And butterflies desire. . . .

A swarm of butterflies! A *storm* of butterflies!

I stepped out on my deck to look at the stars and consider the butterfly. The butterfly ring I had bought to symbolize who I am. The butterfly dance I had done in multicolored scarves and tights and leotard in a personal growth seminar. The picture of the woman with huge butterfly wings under the word "LIFE" that is framed on the wall of my bathroom. The light blue butterflies that were embroidered on the edges of the filmy white scarf that Emily and I bought to cover Katy's arms in the coffin so the IV punctures would not show. The stunningly beautiful blue butterfly that landed on the railing of my deck a couple of days after the funeral and stayed and stayed and stayed. Butterflies, I know, are believed to carry spiritual messages between the living and the dead, and the Greek word for butterfly is the same as the word for soul. The butterfly is the only creature that changes its DNA in the process of transformation; the one that flies from the chrysalis is not the same being as the one that entered.

And remembering Katy, I flashed on the inside cover of the book that had started this storm of butterflies. In slanted, first-grade printing, "This book belongs to Katy Pearson."

And then the inscription inside the book that had ended the storm of butterflies. "For Katy—may you respond to the poetry of your own soul and others. All love from your Mother and her friend Emily Dickinson." A gift from last Christmas. A gift given and returned.

I consider the butterfly. The fragile cocoon falls away. The wings spread and, ah—such beauty! Amen.

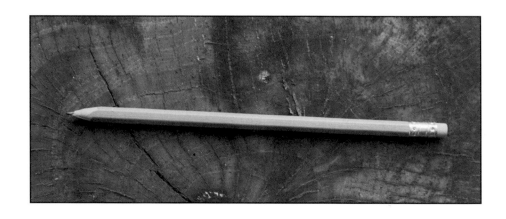

Little Lessons

THE DAILY CLASSROOM.

Recess, vacation, singing time. And always the lesson. Books, paper, pencils, chalkboard, explanation, example, story. And frequently that wonderful field trip into the territory of synchronicity—personal experience tailor-made and unmistakable.

Education from a master teacher.

I Look Just Like Julie's Dog!

Whatever this synchronicity thing is, it has a wild sense of humor.

When I opened an e-mail from my friend Lane and found pictures of the winners of the "I Look Like My Dog" contest, I had to laugh at the uncanny canine-human resemblance:

The man and his bulldog, both bald and round and thick with suspicious eyes and downturned mouths.

The young woman and her cocker spaniel, her wavy hair and his wavy ears, both blond-red, looking like they'd been spun by the same wigmaker.

The young man and his greyhound, both looking disdainfully down their long, thin noses.

The older man and his schnauzer, both with hair parted in the middle, the saddest eyes on the planet, and the weight of the world pulling eyebrows and cheeks down, down, down.

The matron and her beagle, both with expectant dark eyes, and hair and ears bobbed to match.

The older woman with her full grey perm and perky smile, a dead ringer for her poodle.

I sent the e-mail of the dogs and their owners to a few people I thought might get a kick out of them.

That night Rozan called. "Well, we did it again," she said, laughing. "You and I created another synchronicity. Yesterday after school Julie came over and we were just talking." I had met Julie a few months ago, a dynamic, attractive young woman who teaches with Rozan. "She had Bea with her." I had met Bea as well, a small, adorable dog with silky white curly hair. "We got to talking about how Julie is tall and dark and she and Bea don't look at all like they belong together. 'In fact,' I said, 'you know who Bea looks like she belongs with?' I picked up a copy of your video with your picture on the cover when you had the perm. 'Look!' I said. We both just about fell over laughing. The curly white hair, the pretty, sweet face—"

"Rozan, you are kidding me!"

"—the big, earnest eyes. And *then*—"

"And then you opened my e-mail!" I was shouting in disbelief.

"You win! You win the contest! You look just like Julie's dog! And you've got a picture at your house, remember? One time when you and Julie were up here I took a picture of Bea with everybody who was there, and I gave you yours, I know."

I ran downstairs and checked the cabinet where I put photos. There it was! Me holding sweet little Bea in front of me, my chin resting on her head. If only I still had my perm! I reached for a copy of my video and laid the photo against the picture Rozan had used in her comparison.

Oh, yes! Oh, absolutely! My white, curly hair in the same shape as the dog's white silky ears, the sweet face, the big earnest eyes, appearing even to be blue. Something almost ethereal about both. I rolled on the floor in hysterics. I look just like Julie's dog! I do! The winner of the "I Look Like My Dog" contest—is *me!*

Of course, my friend Mario had to make a major metaphysical thing out of it. We had laughed at the joke about the agnostic dyslexic amnesiac who lies awake nights worrying whether or not there's a dog. We had played with the words a number of times—dog and God— whenever it served a transcendent, meaningful purpose. "You know," he said when he finished laughing, "you know, people do look like their gods, that's for sure."

True. And the gods come to look like their people. It's been that way through recorded history. That became clear as I did the research for my one-woman play, *Mother Wove the Morning*, a play that follows the loss of the female face of God, the play on the video of me with my perm and my sweet face and my big earnest eyes. On my shelf now, among many books on the subject, is one by Patricia Lynn Reilly with yearning in its title, *A God Who Looks Like Me*.

That's Mario's take on it. But this time I'm just going to laugh. Laughing is so—so godly!

Maybe even—dogly.

ALI BABA AND SCHEHERAZADE

Sunday evening, and *The Arabian Nights* was on television. Scheherazade. Of course! *That's* where the name comes from! Two days earlier I had called Maria's hair salon for an appointment, and Maria, who usually cuts my hair, was gone. "I can give you a cut this afternoon at two," said the voice with an exotic accent. "This is Scheherazade."

"Great," I said, "I'll be there at two."

Scheherazade, Scheherazade, why couldn't I remember where the name belonged in literature? Somewhere in the ancient East. Clearly I was losing brain cells.

Odd that I should meet the local Scheherazade two days ago and now see the one from literature on my television screen. On the chance that this was a synchronistic invitation, I settled in to watch the made-for-television movie. The Sultan Shahriyar marries many women, then has each one of them strangled the next morning. Our heroine Scheherazade, daughter of the grand vizier, offers to marry the Sultan, and on the day of the wedding gets him to listen to a story. She comes to the most exciting part. "And then—" She stops.

"And then—what?" The Sultan is riveted.

"Tomorrow. I will finish the story tomorrow."

Suspense buys her another day in which to finish the story and cleverly begin another one. And another day to do the same. One thousand and one days, one thousand and one stories.

Commercial break, and I automatically jumped from my chair. I had discovered that I could scrub a toilet or clean two mirrors or do any number of small tasks during a two-minute commercial. The plan now was to run downstairs and locate my actor's copy of *J. B.*, as I wanted to compare the playbook copy ending with the ending in the hardback version of the play Rozan had found for me at the garage sale as the one she gave me did not read quite as I remembered. Hurrying to the large oak bookcase that covers an entire wall, I stood before the drama section and scanned the playbooks. Pulled out one, blue, loose cover. No. Pulled out a second, yellow, no, no, it wasn't yellow. Pulled out a third, grey. Yes. "J. B.—A Play in Verse—by Archibald MacLeish." I grabbed it and ran upstairs.

Back to the first story Scheherazade is telling—"Ali Baba and the Forty Thieves."

"Open sesame!" Another opening slowly grew, that opening I had become so familiar with that said, "Pay attention—two things just collided." Ali Baba . . . ? I had just read the words. Where? On a playbook. A blue playbook with a loose cover!

Without waiting for the next commercial, I ran downstairs to the bookcase. That *first* playbook I had pulled out, the wrong one, right about here. Yes, blue and with a loose cover. I pulled it out. "Ali Baba and the Forty Thieves—dramatized from the Arabian Nights—Price 75 cents." A children's play I had performed in high school, forty-five years ago!

I stand in the cave of my mind tonight as I write this, just as I did the night it happened, examining the possible treasures. Story, the importance of story. I, like Scheherazade, am a storyteller. Her stories saved her life, saved many lives, made the Sultan love her, brought peace to the land. A story can do that. Some of my stories have brought life, love, and peace. Open sesame. There are hidden riches, there are caves, if only I knew the password. But not a stolen password, not a borrowed one, a legitimate one, mine. One that I can speak openly, in confidence. Magical, no. Miraculous, yes. Not in the past, not in the drama of high school. Today. Now. I know there are spaces I need to enter, riches waiting. I know the richest space is within me. I know a mantra is a password that opens. Prayer opens. Intention opens.

Story. I write my little stories, but am living a bigger story, with plot points and a theme. Who is telling my story? A larger-than-life Scheherazade in the sky? A private little Scheherazade in my mind, myself? Do I make it up as I go? Was the outline written by God and me before I was introduced on page one?

Whatever Scheherazade is telling my story, she's got me hooked. While I wrote these pages, the sky turned from blue to black and I see two points of light—my writing candle and the street lamp outside my window. This day is done, and the night brings a suspenseful pause. *And then what? And then what?* What dream will I have tonight? Who will call on the telephone tomorrow? Who will I decide to call? What will be in the mail? What new thought will occur to me as I do my morning hike in the hills? What will be on the pages of the book I am reading? What new complication will erupt into the plot of my life that will require all the strength of my heart? What resolution will come to end years of yearning? What new characters will be introduced? What new light will illuminate the theme? What lesson will I finally learn?

The storytelling is working. I am hooked.

A Libra Such as I

I am a Libra, she with hands held out like the scales of judgment, always saying, "Well, on the one hand there's this, and on the other hand there's that."

New Year's Day. I had spent an hour in my room putting away Christmas presents and tidying the walk-in closet. A whole pile of sweaters and pants were lying on the chest of drawers, and behind them was a lovely, large poster Jan gave me years ago. Ah, with the piles put away I could see it again. I really ought to pay more attention to it, I thought. I've just let it become like wallpaper that I don't notice. And it's so inspiring, really. I should look at it every morning when I'm in here getting dressed.

So much for the closet. Now the family room. Tree gone, decorations put away. I pulled out what I had stuffed under the fireplace ledge to make room for the Christmas things.

What's this one? Oh, yes. That old scale. I had found it years ago at a garage sale and thought, "Oh, a Libra thing! That's me! I need that!" I'd held onto it, displaying it here and there, usually on the mantelpiece or the fireplace ledge. A square wooden base held a carved wooden pole that held a kind of fancy metalwork top from which hung two metal chains that held in balance two round wooden plates. But the pieces had never fit together without leaning a bit. It had a kind of a seventies look and was not very attractive. Still, it was me! It was my Libra thing!

But as I brought it out, I heard myself say out loud, "Why am I keeping this? It's ugly and dark and doesn't stand up straight, and it doesn't do anything for me." I waited for my inner voice to say, "But it's *you!*—it's your *Libra thing!*" But I didn't hear it.

"Okay," I spoke out loud again, standing up. "That's it. Out to the Goodwill box. No. Better plan. I'll see if Rozan would like you for a prop for her drama department at school." I took my ugly, dark, wooden, seventies Libra thing to the front door and placed it on the floor.

Minutes later, I was right in the middle of mindlessly wiping the counter with Pine-Sol and my two sponges (my daughter Emily says I'm the only woman she knows that cleans with a sponge in each hand, but after all, I am a Libra—in the one hand there's this, in the other hand there's that), when I froze. Upstairs, just a few minutes before, in my closet—.

I put down my sponges, walked up the stairs, down the hall, into my bedroom, and stopped in my walk-in closet. Yes! Oh, beautiful! Oh, *perfect!* The poster Jan gave me years ago that I was admiring after I got my stuff out from in front of it. I had stood there thinking I should pay more attention to this. Yes, the beautiful purple border, I had said to myself, yes, that's the color that I see when I meditate, rolling in and out of that other darkish-pinkish color they've used to spell out the word, "L-i-b-r-a." And yes, the beautiful face of the woman with the blindfold, very calm, strong, sweet. And yes, I had thought, that rod above her head, resting in the tree of life that grows from her forehead, holding the scales above her shoulders. I had never noticed that in one scale was the sun and in the other the moon. Ah, I've been doing that, I had thought, working on balancing my sun and my moon, my yin and my yang. And the lotus opening at her throat. Yes, I should pay more attention to this, study it every morning as I'm getting dressed, let it inspire me. Those were the thoughts I'd had only minutes ago about this beautiful, beautiful Libra thing!

New Year's Day. A good day to throw out the old and bring in the new. Throw out what is dark and not very attractive and won't stand up straight and has been in the way and does not inspire. Recommit to what the soul chooses with its automatic, infallible response beauty, light, grace, meaning, balance. Perfect, perfect balance.

I did give the old, dark, wooden scales to Rozan.

"Sure!" she said, when I asked if she could use it for drama class. "It'd be a great prop."

The next morning at nine-thirty, my phone rang. "Carol Lynn? I'm at school. You won't *believe* this! First period one of my students comes up to me and says, 'Mrs. Gautier, for our scene, we need one of those balance scales. You don't have one of those balance scales, do you?' In all my years of teaching, no one has *ever* asked me for scales!"

The old balance scales is exactly where it needs to be, in the theatre, the world of illusion.

And I, excellent Libra that I am, am exactly where I need to be, dressing every morning in front of beauty and light and perfect balance, the world of reality.

I brought the beautiful Libra poster in and propped it up on a chair so I could look at it while I wrote this piece. I've been writing as fast as I can because I promised Rozan that at three I would go with her and

Brad to have some fun. When she called this sunny Saturday morning and said, "Hey, Brad and I decided to go over to Oakland to see the 'Forbidden City' exhibit at the museum, get a bite to eat, and then go see *Chocolat*. Want to come?"—my first thought was, "Oh, gee, I've planned to write that good Libra piece today . . . "

But on the other hand, I know that I *need* a little fun. It really would be *good* for me.

COMMUNICATION CRUSHED

There was the squeak of the mailbox. All right! A small padded package in my friend Neal's handwriting. For years the tape recorder had been our communication tool of choice, and we loved taking turns at a conversation that went on forever like a slow tennis match. Stories, philosophies, jokes. I opened the package and an envelope fell out, the kind of envelope I was so used to seeing in our correspondence. It had been postmarked a month before and a large "Return to Sender" had been stamped on it, with the printed explanation, "Odd-shaped items are not mailable in letter style envelopes, because they could burst the envelope and damage mail-processing equipment or injure employees." WHAT?

I called the next morning to tell Neal I'd finally received the ill-fated tape. "So what about that stupid return thing?" I asked. "We've been sending tapes to each other for years, just inside cards, and not one has ever been damaged. They just want to get more postage out of us."

I hung up the phone and went immediately to check my e-mail. A message from my daughter Emily.

The tape you sent us of your last talk in church was broken
in pieces when we opened it. Do you want to try again?
I love you very much, Mom. XOXO, Em

I sent another copy of the tape to Emily. In a padded envelope.
And a tape with some most interesting stories to Neal. In a padded
envelope. But I knew that was just the first layer of meaning in this
remarkable coincidence. There was definitely a metaphor here.
Communication is a very fragile thing. It needs protecting. How
often I have seen the effects of communication without care, without
reverence, without protection. What about my communications? Are
there misunderstandings that need to be cleared up? Words that need
to be spoken, spoken carefully?

This morning I got a call from Emily. "Mom? The kids and I were in
a car accident last night. Don't panic, we're okay. The woman behind
me was dialing her cell phone. . . ." A cut on Tara's toe. Bruises. A
strained back. The car, totaled. After a prayer of gratitude, I went about
my morning, finished the crushed tape story. Fragile. Life is so fragile.
Bodies so fragile. Communication so fragile. "So glad we were in the big
van." The tape in pieces, needed padding. The car totaled.

My communication with Emily secure? Yes. With all others? No. One
of my children leaps out at me. This weekend I will have an opportunity
to be with that one for two days. There are words that need to be said,
misunderstandings that need to be cleared, apologies that need to be
made, love that needs to be spoken. I will try to do it well and carefully.
Communication, I know, is fragile. It deserves protection.

"I Fear I Have Stolen My Potatoes!"

Time for a major shopping trip. I was picking up my daughter Emily at the airport at noon and she had said, "Oh, I'm looking forward to eating healthy this weekend. I've been eating such junk. I want salads, salads, salads, and, of course, your apple pie."

I hurried through the aisles at Safeway, then headed to the produce section. Lettuce, spinach, tomatoes, purple onion. A policeman in uniform. *Three* policemen in uniform, quietly discussing the produce. Automatically I glanced away. Am I speeding? Is my registration tag up to date? Dumb. And the poor guys would probably like to be treated like normal people.

I looked directly at them and smiled. "Hiya, Officers. How're you doing?"

"Great," one of them replied. "Are we in your way here?"

I laughed. "Are you kidding? And even if you were, who would *ever* say so?"

I picked up a ten-pound bag of potatoes and slid it on the rack under the cart, then hurried to the checkout counter.

"Need any help out with that?"

"No, thanks, Bruce, I've got it." I always read people's tags and call them by name.

I quickly rolled the cart out of the store, threw the bags into my van, and lifted the ten-pound bag of potatoes from underneath. Uh oh. The potatoes. I did not have a kinesthetic memory of lifting the potatoes up and placing them on the conveyor belt. Had I not paid for my potatoes?

I grabbed my purse and pulled out the Safeway receipt, scanning it hurriedly. Potatoes, potatoes, potatoes. *No potatoes!* I had not paid for my potatoes! I glanced at the store—and saw *three policemen heading right for me!* Stifling a laugh, I looked from my receipt to the officers.

"What's the matter?" asked the one that had talked before. "Didn't they do it right?"

"Oh, Officers," I said with an embarrassed giggle, "I fear—I have *stolen my potatoes!*"

I'm not sure what I expected them to do—haul me up against my van and pat me down for concealed radishes? But what they *did* do surprised the heck out of me.

The officer who talked waved it all away, saying, "Ah, it was a freebie."

Confused, I turned toward them as they passed. "But—but, no, it's not a freebie. It's not."

I ran the hot potatoes (oh, very funny) back into the store. "Bruce," I said, "I'm sorry, but—I fear I have stolen my potatoes." He thanked me and took my two dollars.

On the way home I couldn't stop giggling. But I was a little disappointed too. I had just stolen potatoes and an officer of the law had told me it was okay! What did *that* mean? I guess to remember that there is a higher law. Always, always listen to the voice inside.

There's one more thing, which I am adding now some weeks later. The other day I went back to Safeway for the first time since my potato heist. I was hurrying through the produce section when a sign caught my eye. "Ten Pounds Potatoes—Buy One, Get One Free."

Well, okay! Do it right and you get your freebie after all!

—◌

From Darkness into Light

"PEACE, BE STILL."

Like the Master calming the storm, my little messages speak comfort to me when my soul is tossed. Come out of the anguish, the doubt. Do not fear. You are not alone. The Universe that God created is a wise and compassionate place. Laugh, even.

I do not find a message that condemns me, condemns others, or suggests that life is a dark event.

The little rips in the mortal curtain let in just enough light to presage that splendid all-encompassing Love that is the world we do not see.

A GIFT OF POTS

It rained all day yesterday. I wrote "Mama's Cinnamon Rolls." I meditated. I took care of business calls and letters. But I missed my morning walk in the hills, such a great way to start the day. Finally about six, the sky cleared and I jumped at the opportunity of walking to the park. As I stepped onto the porch and pulled my red hooded sweatshirt over my head, my gaze fell onto the half-dozen plants arranged beside the door. My young friend Xan had needed someone to plant-sit while she spent four months in China studying various Eastern healing practices. Several plants were inside the house, but these particular ones seemed to want more daylight and so they had found a home here on the porch. I had become used to watering them and encouraging their thriving, and appreciating the welcome they gave me in my comings and goings. I had forgotten they were only here on loan.

Xan was coming back in two weeks. For the first time I connected that with the plants on the porch. "Darn," I said to myself, as I moved down the sidewalk. "Of course she'll be taking the plants back. Too bad. I will miss them."

Forty minutes later, exhilarated now from my walk and just a few houses away from home, I was suddenly brought out of my walking reverie by a voice saying, "Hi, Mrs. Pearson."

"Oh, hello, Roy." It had been a few years since I had seen this gentle boy that my children had grown up with, now tall but still redheaded and shyly smiling. "What are you up to?"

"Just helping my folks get the house ready. They're moving to San Diego. Say, do you need any pots? My dad did a lot of pottery. Here, let me show you."

He led me to the side of the house, where I saw perhaps a hundred pots in all sizes and shapes and colors, raindrops still glistening on their glazed bellies.

"Help yourself if you see anything you'd like."

"Gee, thanks, Roy. I will."

Minutes later I continued on my way, my arms now heavy with four fine clay pots, blue, grey, a bit of mottled green—excellent for the colors in my home.

I stepped onto the porch and directly into my "synchronicity space." When last I had stood here, I was considering the loss of the plants. And now, I held in my arms a gift of pots to house new ones.

Empty vessels to hold new life. Space to invite growing and greening. I had spent the week mourning the loss of something huge and rooted so deeply that letting it go tore the earth of my heart. It seems it was here only on loan.

But there is space now. My heart is an empty vessel, and yes, it has been shaped at the wheel and fired. I will invite new life. I will ask for green.

And when it stops raining, I will go out and buy four new plants.

STOP AND START

So tired. I had lain awake most of the night staring at the ceiling, racked with concern. This morning I made myself walk to the park. Coming back, despite the warm sun and the cheery bird calls, I found myself spiraling down, down, my usual strength giving way like a burst dam, too tired to fight the rushing darkness, allowing the worst possible scenario to play out in my mind.

"Stop!" The voice was loud and sure. It was my own voice. I was standing still on the path, my eyes closed, hearing myself sharply insist, "Stop!" I took a few breaths and opened my eyes. The first thing that appeared in my vision was a word, a word in large, white block letters only ten feet away from me on the asphalt path: STOP. The path was about to meet the street. But I had been about to meet the abyss.

A warning sign.

Hours later, I was leaving my granddaughters' elementary school, where I had been with both the kindergarten and first grade classes, doing "creative drama" with Aesop's fables. Still tired, I was hurrying to my car, cutting across the schoolyard. There, under my feet, what was I standing on? A word. A word in large, white block letters on the asphalt playground: START.

Start? Playing? Learning? Becoming a child? Trusting?

An invitation.

CONNECTED TO MY SOLE

Should I be surprised at the synchronicity that *my synchronicities and I* share the trait of loving to play with language, even making puns? Or that we share another trait, walking a constant fine line between laughter and tears?

I must tell you about the hearts, the tiny red hearts. A couple of years ago my son John sent me a birthday card that had inside it a thick layer of tiny red glittering hearts. As I opened the card, the hearts sprayed everywhere, covering my lap and the carpet with little glints of love. Loath to consign this sweetness to the vacuum, I let the hearts stay for a few days, then a few days longer. They spread. Now there were some on the stairway, now downstairs in the front room, here in the kitchen, there on the porch. My feet carried them everywhere.

When my two granddaughters came for the weekend, I had them

close their eyes and said, "Guess who came to my house last week?"

"Who?" they demanded.

"The Love Fairy! And look what she left!"

They opened their eyes to hundreds of little red hearts winking from the carpet.

"Oh, wow!" And they dove down to harvest the hearts. But even after they had picked up every visible one, we continued to find them. The girls would come running with a tiny red heart pressed into a finger. "Look, Grandma Blossom. I am loved!"

I would find them on my own, in the strangest places, and say to myself, oh, look, I am loved. They were there in my bedding, in the drain of my bathtub, in the washing machine, in a crack in the sidewalk, in the silverware drawer, in the ashes of my gas log. I even found one floating in my hot tub. Ah, yes, I am loved.

One evening I was getting ready to go up to Rozan's for a meeting of church business. I chose to wear a white shirt with Levi's, grabbed my white walking shoes, then paused. No, I don't want to wear these shoes. This is just a casual event with some women friends, but I feel like pretending that it's not. I want to pretend I'm going out with a man I love.

No mystery there. I had spent some time that day going through parts of my diary, reviewing the synchronicities that would make good stories for this book. In doing so, I had tracked a series of spectacular synchronicities that I had shared with the man whose love had completely transformed me, been rain and sun to my growth as a woman. A starcrossed love that lived daily in my heart, wrapped in both joy and grief.

Tonight I was feeling more of the joy than the grief, and I thought, okay, what shoes would I wear if I were going to be with my love tonight? Of course. I picked up the black sandals that consisted of a thin sole with fishnet to cover the foot. Very sexy shoes. In fact, I believed the last time I had worn them was the last time I had been with my star-crossed love, the time I believed would be the last I would ever see him.

Before I began dressing, I had put on some music. Feeling mellow, I had chosen a CD called *Shaina Noll: Songs for the Inner Child*, very sweet, simple, spiritually comforting songs. As I write this now, I look at the cover and see that it was produced by Singing Heart Productions and that each of the songs listed has a tiny heart beside it. The first song was my favorite.

How could anyone ever tell you you were anything
less than beautiful?
How could anyone ever tell you you were less than whole?

I placed the black sandals on the carpet and was about to put them on. Something was on the sole of the left sandal. A little red heart smiling up at me.

How could anyone fail to notice that your loving is a miracle?

Something was on the leather sole of the *right* sandal. A matching little red heart! A heart pressed into the sole of each of my sandals, a little memento from the last time I had been with my love.

How deeply you're connected to my soul!

Suddenly the words of the song were dancing in synch with the black sandals I held in my hands with the little red hearts pressed into the soles.

How deeply you're connected to my sole!

Oh, deeply. Connected more deeply, pressed more deeply into my soul than the glittering hearts could ever be pressed into leather. I could never fail to notice. Your loving is a miracle. How deeply, deeply and always you're connected to my soul.

GOD'S ALCHEMY

Yesterday I wrote the story of the sole/soul connection. Last night I went to bed wrapped more in the grief of it than the joy of it, the enigma of this splendid, star-crossed love. Why this wondrous promise forever unfulfilled? Why? I lay in bed praying out loud. *Please, just help me to understand.* I woke several times in the night with the same prayer. *Help me to understand!*

Morning comes. I open *A Course in Miracles*, page 591: ". . . all things must be first forgiven, and *then* understood." Forgiveness. It's not that I forget about forgiveness. It's just easier to remember on good days, like it's easier to remember sunlight at noon than in the middle of the night. Yes, I remember forgiveness. It's the foundation of my spiritual construct. So hard I have worked to forgive. Today I forgive again, and will again tomorrow. When I have truly forgiven, then, then will I understand?

Rozan and I had spent the evening with our girls at Anderson House, all deeply wounded from life's most brutal blows. Last week we had decided to do "gratitude journals" and Rozan had bought attractive little journals and pens, asking each girl to write down five small things of the day she could be grateful for. "Anyone care to share?" she asked.

Hannah, a sweet-faced fifteen year-old who had gained seventy pounds in the last six months, taken out of her family three weeks ago because of ongoing sexual abuse from a brother, raised her hand. "I'll read one," she said softly. "I'm grateful that today for the first time in months I looked in the mirror and I said, 'You are beautiful.'"

"Oh! And you are!" I reached over and ran my hand along her cheek.

So now, preparing my little supper, I was thinking about Hannah. How can I see any of this as good? I began a tentative dialogue with her in my mind. "Hannah, what happened to you was not okay. It should never have happened. But—but it did happen. And somehow, in a way that I do not understand, bad things can be turned into good things."

That's as far as I got. I was not satisfied.

I took my plate upstairs to watch TV while I ate. No, not CNN with the interminable recount of votes in Florida. What's this one? Biblical. Joseph in Egypt embraces a brother. The brother speaks. "No, no, we do not deserve your forgiveness. We sold you into slavery."

Joseph speaks. "The Lord brought me to Egypt. It was his plan so that I can now save my family from the famine."

Clicking off the TV, I ate in silence. The Lord brought Joseph to Egypt. Something bad was turned into something good. Joseph's brothers sold him into slavery. That should not have happened. Hannah's brother sold her into slavery, took away her autonomy, her freedom, her precious sense of self. That should not have happened. Is Hannah in a land of Egypt where she can somehow, someday, turn wrong into benefit, receiving tenfold what has been taken away?

Later I sat in my hot tub, looking at the stars. Always a good place to process the day. Sometimes events and insights moved into a new constellation. ". . . All things must be first forgiven, and *then* understood." Joseph forgave his brothers *first*, I'm sure, and *then* understood the larger plan, *then* saw the alchemy of God that took base metal and turned it into gold. For Hannah, forgiveness and understanding may come. That is between her and God.

What is between *me* and God, clear as that line of stars—little points of light in the dark sky—is trust and forgiveness. Trust that my dreams that were sold into Egypt can someday be redeemed and multiplied. Trust that my grief can be touched by God's alchemy and turned into a shining thing.

First forgiveness. Forgiveness always.

GRATITUDE

Yesterday I wrote the introduction to this book. All of the other sections were written. Such fun to create a beginning. So fun to write the final words—

More than ever before, the Universe has my attention.
And my gratitude.

I blew out my writing candle. My home teachers from church,

David and Diana McClun, were coming for their monthly visit.

A bit cold downstairs. Light the fire. Turn on the Tiffany lamps. Answer the doorbell. Handshakes. Hugs. Chitchat by the fire. Warmth. Laughter. "Our message this month," said David, "is gratitude." Ah, yes, gratitude. That was the last word I wrote, just minutes before.

A discussion of that good subject, more chitchat, warmth, laughter, a prayer, another handshake, and hug, and a promise that yes, I would consider gratitude.

And so I considered gratitude as I climbed into bed last night. Perhaps I should write one final story for the book on today's sweet, subtle synchronicity of gratitude. Plus, it would tie the ending back to the beginning, and I like that idea.

This morning before climbing into the shower, anxious to get to my writing, I put into my tape recorder the final tape of Deepak's *SynchroDestiny* set that I was listening to again, and turned it up loud enough to hear over the spraying water. He began by saying that in the Middle Ages, when commentaries on the Bible were being written, it was thought that

. . . the end of the book was supposed to connect back to the beginning. The last part should lead back into the first thought again. So in theory you could just keep reading the book over and over again. There might be a last page to the volume, but there was no real end to the book. . . . The universe itself is basically circular in form rather than linear. There's a unity and a harmony that suggests a circle rather than a line. . . a dance, the cosmic dance.